Igor Stravinsky

Titles in the series Critical Lives present the work of leading cultural figures of the modern period. Each book explores the life of the artist, writer, philosopher or architect in question and relates it to their major works.

In the same series

Igor Stravinsky

Jonathan Cross

REAKTION BOOKS

In memoriam John Everill Cross (1930–2014)

Published by Reaktion Books Ltd
Unit 32, Waterside
33–48 Wharf Road
London N1 7UX, UK

www.reaktionbooks.co.uk

First published 2015, reprinted 2017

Copyright © Jonathan Cross 2015

Printed and bound in Great Britain
by Bell & Bain, Glasgow

A catalogue record for this book is available from the British Library

ISBN 978 1 78023 494 6

Contents

Igor Stravinsky, *c.* 1930.

Preface: Finding Igor

Think of a symbol of Russia, of the Russian folk. What first springs to mind? Most likely a wooden doll, nested inside a number of other wooden dolls of gradually increasing size, decorated as a peasant girl or woman with black eyes and sharply etched eyelashes, rosy red cheeks, and always wearing a headscarf and apron emblazoned with bright flowers. This is матрёшка, the *matryoshka*. Matryona or Matriosha was a common peasant-girl's name. At the root of the word is the Latin *mater*, related to the modern Russian words for mother, *mat'*, *matushka*. For the Russian, then, the *matryoshka* is intimately linked to the image of mother and motherhood, and thence to the notion of Russia as motherland. Rooted in the skills and traditions of an ancient people in touch with the earth, these little wooden dolls stand for an enduring idea of Rus'. For the outsider, the *matryoshka* doll has also often been read as a symbol of the inscrutable Russian mind: in Winston Churchill's famous phrase, uttered at the outbreak of the Second World War, Russia 'is a riddle wrapped in a mystery inside an enigma'.

It is certainly true that there was a long tradition of woodworking in Russia. One famous centre of folk art was the city of Sergiev Posad, which lies about 70 kilometres north of Moscow. The 'first Sergiev Posad toy was made in the 13th century by St Sergius of Radonezh . . . [The] tsar's children received toys from Sergiev Posad as early as 1628 . . . [and by] 1880, there were 322 toy workshops in Sergiev Posad'.[1] But no *matryoshki*. The *matryoshka* doll as it is now known first appeared in Sergiev Posad only in 1899.[2] The idea for a nested doll actually came from a Japanese import. It is generally accepted that the first Russian *matryoshka* doll was made and painted in the Abramtsevo workshop, an artists' colony founded on an estate just outside Sergiev Posad by the wealthy railway magnate Savva Mamontov and his wife Elizaveta. Abramtsevo became a crucible for art, for opera, and for the encouragement of a neo-nationalist Russian aesthetic. The *matryoshka*, though rooted in peasant crafts, was born of both an aristocratic and a modern desire to preserve a rapidly vanishing past and to sell this idea of Russia to a wider public. The doll became an object of international desire when, in 1900, an example was exhibited at the Exposition Universelle in Paris alongside other Russian folk art. It won an award, and the orders soon started to flood in, keeping generations of Russian artisans in employment. One travelling Russian who was at the exhibition, and who saw the doll there, was a man by the name of Sergey Diaghilev. It prompted him to think that this enthusiasm in Paris for the import of iconic Russian objects might extend beyond mass-produced wooden figurines.

So, it turns out that what in the West has come to be identified with an authentic expression of the ancient Russian folk spirit is in fact an invention prompted by those potent twins of modernity: nostalgia and commerce.

In 1898, just a year before the *matryoshka*, a group of well-to-do young St Petersburg artists and thinkers, under the leadership of Diaghilev, made a dramatic public debut under the banner of *Mir iskusstva*, the 'World of Art', a journal and movement devoted to the radical presentation of a neo-Russian art derived from folk traditions. Some of them had even had contact with Abramtsevo. Their influence on the early Igor Stravinsky was to prove decisive. Within just one decade, Stravinsky and his collaborators had taken

Panoramic view of the Exposition Universelle, Paris, 1900.

the stories, art and music of Old Russia and refashioned them into a ballet for export to Paris. The French adored the glamour, colour and invented authenticity of the firebird. They embraced her in just the same way they had the *matryoshka*. And they embraced Stravinsky too, who went on to make France his home, to reinvent himself as a Frenchman, and to present a new kind of French attitude in his music in keeping with a changed climate after the First World War. Decades later, this doll too was twisted open and pulled apart to reveal an American Stravinsky, speaking yet another new language in deference to his hosts.

To write a biography of Igor Stravinsky, the master of self-reinvention, is an impossible task. True, the broad facts and habits of the life are now well known, thanks to the painstaking work of distinguished scholars who have devoted their careers to the study of archives full of correspondence, diaries, sketches, contracts, medical and legal bills, and the other paraphernalia of a life, seeking evidence to confirm or refute the public utterances of the man himself, his family, his supporters and his apologists. Yet many unknowns, uncertainties and contradictions still remain. Even the testimony of those – living and dead – who knew the man well, are not entirely to be trusted, since the stories they tell are inconsistent. So where should we look to find the 'real' Igor Stravinsky? And how will we recognize him when we see him?

Like the *matryoshka*, Stravinsky was born into a rapidly changing world. During his lifetime the country of his birth was transformed almost beyond recognition. Stravinsky observed this mainly from afar, as an émigré, but war and revolution, illness and death nonetheless left their wounds. He rarely spoke about such matters. But the wounds are undoubtedly there, and they can be heard in the music he created. Like the *matryoshka*, his art was born of nostalgia, nostalgia for a lost Russia, for a Russia perhaps of the imagination, but a Russia which formed him, and which he turned to modern purpose, to speak (it should be said, with some commercial success) to a world equally touched by experiences of loss. Stravinsky's was just one life lived against a backdrop of tumultuous times. His music in subtle and complex ways registers this life such that others, too, might recognize their own responses in it.

One can never be certain, even when on the rare occasion Stravinsky appears to be speaking genuinely. After all, he once famously declared (or, rather, the ghostwriter of his autobiography did) that music is incapable of expressing anything at all. How can we really know if this lament or that expression of love is authentic? Is the listener being duped? Does this matter? Maybe there is no authentic Stravinsky to be found. What does the music tell of an authentic Stravinsky? What does the *matryoshka* tell of an authentic Russia? Maybe all we have is 'Stravinsky', an invention of his and others' making. But this very invention is itself a product of a time and place. In looking for the connections between the man, his times and his art, my ambition for this 'critical life' is simply to try to say something about how and why the music of Igor Stravinsky speaks so powerfully of its age.

Prelude: How Stravinsky Became 'Stravinsky'

Good Friday, 9 April 1971. In New York City, at the corner of
Madison Avenue and 81st Street, outside Frank E. Campbell's
dour but well-kept funeral home for the rich and famous, a crowd
has been gathering steadily since at least midday. Reporters,
photographers, music lovers and many more besides stand in
respectful silence. Some have travelled great distances to be present.
They have come to pay homage to a great musician, whose solemn
funeral services are about to begin in the mortuary chapel. Taking
their place on the pavement are two European composers in their
mid-forties, one called Luciano (Berio), the other called André
(Boucourechliev), whose own music owes an immeasurable debt to
the work of the recently departed. They exchange occasional glances
as they strain to catch a glimpse of the proceedings through the
open doors. A young student, who never knew the deceased but
still feels a deep need just to be there that cold, spring afternoon,
speaks haltingly to a correspondent from the *New York Times*:
'This is my way of showing what his music meant to me.'

   At a little before 3 pm, the widow arrives on the arm of the aide
and closest friend of the deceased, parting the patiently waiting
throng. They quickly make their way inside and are ushered to the
front row of the chapel, on the right. On the left-hand side, their
distance painfully expressing the strained state of family relations
of late, sit the composer's surviving daughter, his two sons and
their wives, a grandson and a granddaughter. At the last moment

a representative of the composer's publisher rushes to take her place next to the widow, gesturing as she does to the relatives on the other side of the aisle. The service begins with sounds the composer himself had made. *'Otche nash . . .'*, the choir gently intones in the ancient Slavonic tongue: 'Our father, which art in heaven . . .'. In this moment, the apparent chasm between the old Russian world of the man's birth and the modern American world of his death seems instantly to be bridged.

The composer whose life had quietly ebbed away just three days earlier was Igor Fyodorovich Stravinsky. The silence of his passing at 5.20 am on 6 April in his newly purchased ten-room apartment on Fifth Avenue stood in stark contrast to the cacophony of the worldwide reaction that followed. The composer's personal manager, it is said, had been hard at work from the moment he died, and the story of the great composer's demise was already making headline news on some of the 6 am broadcasts that day. The apartment was soon inundated with telegrams, messages of condolence, flowers, telephone calls. A supremely private moment rapidly became a public event. The whole world, it seemed, felt they owned Stravinsky, as the papers across the globe made clear the following day. 'Unmistakably, he was the towering figure in twentieth century music', pronounced Edward Greenfield on the front page of *The Guardian.* Paul Hume of the *Washington Post* went further: Stravinsky was 'one of the great, original creative geniuses in the entire history of music'. A leader in the *New York Times* hailed him 'the most modern of the moderns', and a number of news-papers were quick off the mark in garnering tributes from the international greats of the modern music and dance worlds, all of whom knew and had worked with Stravinsky: Otto Klemperer, Leopold Stokowski, Isaac Stern, Leonard Bernstein, Aaron Copland, Virgil Thomson, Frederick Ashton and George Balanchine among them. The influence of Stravinsky, as Harold C. Schonberg proclaimed in the same issue of the *Times*, was 'all embracing'.

That such universalist claims were being made for Stravinsky and his music even before his body had been interred should hardly surprise us. Throughout much of his life, Stravinsky had himself been largely responsible for his representation as a cosmopolitan figure, as someone whose music could speak to all people in a kind of Esperanto that transcended national boundaries and identities. The tone now adopted by his obituarists certainly helped consolidate a view that persists even today, namely that Stravinsky was the last of the 'great composers', that he was a composer of Beethovenian magnitude who spoke 'in the purest language of all peoples' (as Wagner wrote of Beethoven).[1]

In the days following Stravinsky's death, hardly a commentator failed to make reference to *The Rite of Spring*, the one work with which not only the composer but an entire century had come to be identified. The elemental power of its music, along with the oft-repeated story of the riot that accompanied its premiere, has imbued the *Rite* with a revolutionary *élan terrible* that links it directly to Beethoven's *Eroica*, *Fidelio* and Ninth Symphony. Charles Acton, in his eulogy in the *Irish Times* of 7 April, gave explicit voice to such an understanding.

> What can ordinary people write about the immortals? . . . What could one have written faced with the death of Beethoven? For, whatever the verdict on Stravinsky's music may be in 50 or 200 years time, he and the music of this century are related, as were Beethoven and that of the last . . . And surely for mankind as a whole the birth of Beethoven in 1770, and the death of Stravinsky, almost precisely two centuries later, define a period of our history.

He was not the only man with Beethoven on his mind. Robert Craft gives an account of events surrounding the first prayer service for Stravinsky held at Campbell's funeral chapel on the evening of 6 April 1971:

a wondrous thing happens. As we leave the apartment an unseasonable snow begins to fall and the winds to howl. Now, as the Bishop pronounces the name 'Igor', three great bursts of thunder reply, as if Nature were acknowledging the departure from the world of a natural force.[2]

The parallels with reports of Beethoven's death in 1827 are unmistakable.

Monday 26th [March]. Freezing. Frequent snow, north wind. Towards 4 o' clock it darkened. Snow blizzards, thunder and lightening. Nature in revolt. Three terrific thunderclaps followed. Death of Ludwig van Beethoven in the evening towards 6 o' clock from dropsy in his 56th year. He is no more. His name lives in glorious light.[3]

Neither account is verifiable, but then, surely, neither of them is literal. Both accounts imply a universal truth through the divine number three; both ascribe agency to Romantic nature. What greater validation could a great composer need? By such means Beethoven the man became 'Beethoven Hero', and Igor Fyodorovich became 'Stravinsky'. Until his death, many of the details of Stravinsky's biography remained largely unspoken – the philandering, the avarice, the anti-Semitism, the snobbery, the narcissism, the cruelty, the hypochondria, the vulnerability – which is perhaps a little surprising for a man who lived the life of a celebrity composer in an increasingly celebrity-obsessed age. But already in his own lifetime Stravinsky had become 'Stravinsky', and the Romantic notion of the heroic, universal composer was regulating his reception. In the moment of his death, one might say, Stravinsky became another Beethoven.

That the *idea* of Stravinsky already exceeded the *man* is evident if one returns, for a moment, to the mourners in the Madison Avenue chapel on 9 April. In the pews in front of the mahogany coffin sat both Michael Whitney Straight, representative of u.s. president Richard Nixon, deputy chairman of the National Endowment for the Arts and former Soviet spy, and Anatoly Dyuzhev, cultural attaché to the Soviet Embassy in Washington, DC. From the political centres of these opposed Cold War regimes sprang letters of condolence to the widow, Vera Stravinsky. With strong echoes of Beethoven's Ninth, the White House wrote of Stravinsky as

> a giant in the world of music. His brilliant pioneering work
> has helped shape an entire generation of musicians – men
> and women inspired by his creativity and challenged by his
> greatness. Surely, the power and force of his genius help
> to make all men brothers and the magnitude of his loss
> transcends all national boundaries.

And from the Soviet Ministry of Culture, Yekaterina Furtseva wrote:

> With feeling of deepest sorrow, we learned about the death of
> one of the greatest contemporary composers . . . and mourn
> him with you. On behalf of Soviet art workers and myself, [we]
> express most sincere sympathies.

The ideal of the unity and brotherhood of all mankind celebrated in Beethoven and Schiller's 'Ode to Joy' was, it would seem, brought about through Stravinsky's death. Or, rather, one should say that both sides were able to claim Stravinsky as their own since each side saw Stravinsky as representing their own ideological values – ironically enough, because Stravinsky's work had been idealized so as to speak beyond ideology and politics. That Stravinsky was, for much of his life, publicly hostile to his native country and culture, and certainly to the Soviet Union, that he only once, late in life, set foot inside post-Revolutionary Russia, and that his music had even been used in the 1950s by a CIA-funded agency as part of anti-Soviet propaganda was irrelevant to what 'Stravinsky' had become. Like Beethoven's death, Stravinsky's touched many precisely because his music had come to mean something to everyone. Thousands had lined the streets of Vienna to witness Beethoven's funeral procession, as depicted in Franz Stober's famous painting of 1827. In Venice almost a century and a half later, many thousands thronged in and around the flower-clad basilica and *campo* of Santi Giovanni e Paolo for Stravinsky's final funeral ceremony on 15 April, as caught on celluloid by countless paparazzi. As Stravinsky's coffin was borne by gondola to its ultimate resting place on the cemetery island of San Michele, hundreds more watched from the Fondamenta dei Mendicanti and hung from windows and canal bridges. Many knelt in respect and crossed themselves. Once in the open water of the lagoon the cortège was surrounded by a flotilla of photographers and TV crews, each jockeying for position, all clamouring for the best shot. Even as Vera Stravinsky threw the first handful of earth into the open grave, clicking cameras captured the moment from the top of a vine-covered wall overlooking the maestro's final resting place.

The funeral invitation had contained a warm tribute from Giorgio Longo, Mayor of Venice, which was also posted on walls around the city in the traditional Italian manner. 'The City of Venice pays homage to the great musician IGOR STRAVINSKY who with a gesture of exquisite friendship wanted in life to be buried in the city he loved more than any other.' As many have subsequently remarked, this was not entirely true. Yes, he loved Venice, the site of the premiere of, among a number of works, *The Rake's Progress*. But he had never expressed a strong desire to be buried there; that was the decision of others. Yet, given the competing claims of ownership over Stravinsky, Venice was the ideal choice. Neither Los Angeles nor Leningrad would have done, so where better than the city that historically straddled Occident and Orient? A city of canals like his childhood St Petersburg; a city of culture, fashion and extrovert wealth like his adopted Hollywood; a city that seemed always to be looking back to the past, like the man himself. An Orthodox funeral in a Catholic church. A decor and *mise-en-scène* more extravagant than anything Léon Bakst could ever have imagined for the Ballets Russes. Diaghilev had long been resting there and Vera would eventually join him. With hindsight it seems inevitable that it was La Serenissima that would allow Stravinsky to take control of his own image beyond this life in just the way he had tried to manage it so carefully while he was still alive.

Stravinsky's waterborne hearse in front of the basilica of Santi Giovanni e Paulo, Venice, 15 April 1971.

1

A Son of St Petersburg

Situated on the Gulf of Finland some 40 kilometres west of St
Petersburg, the small town of Oranienbaum took its name from
the exotic plants found in the glass houses ('orangeries') of the
gardens of the Grand Palace that had been built there in the early
eighteenth century for Aleksandr Menshikov, adviser to Peter
the Great. It is a glorious piece of Baroque architecture in the
characteristic Germano-Italian manner of Petersburg, sitting
in a landscaped Dutch-style park. It later became the country
residence of both Peter III and Catherine the Great, who in turn
commissioned further buildings for the estate, including a pastiche
castle and Chinese palace. In 1744 the Imperial Porcelain Factory
was established in close proximity, for the manufacture of the
finest chinaware to be used at the imperial Court. This Russian
town with a German name was also to be the birthplace of the
self-styled cosmopolitan Igor Stravinsky, who grew up in Russia
speaking German with his nanny, and who became the composer
of *The Nightingale* (set in part in the Emperor of China's Porcelain
Palace), of *Pulcinella* (based on music of early eighteenth-century
Italian provenance), and of all kinds of neoclassical 'pastiches'
within and across his works. Oranienbaum, then, is a fitting place
to find the story of his life beginning.

Known now as Lomonosov, it was in this town of the orange
tree that Igor Fyodorovich was born in a rented wooden *dacha* to
Fyodor Ignat'yevich Stravinsky and Anna Kirillovna Stravinskaya

(née Kholodovskaya) on 5 June 1882 (in the Old Style Julian calendar, OS). Oranienbaum was in the 1880s a fashionable resort to which the artistic community of Petersburg retreated in the summer months, so it was only natural that the celebrated singer and bibliophile Fyodor should have chosen to take his family there. Musorgsky had been there before them, and it was as Varlaam in that great Russian composer's opera *Boris Godunov* that Fyodor appeared in Oranienbaum's ninteenth-century theatre. By the time of Igor's birth the family's primary home was on the Kryukov Canal in St Petersburg, building number 8 – in apartment number 66 on the second floor – which was situated opposite the Mariinsky Theatre, home of the Imperial Opera. Fyodor had been engaged there as one of the principal basses since 1876. Over the course of the next quarter of a century he appeared in more than 60 roles, ranging from the lyrical Italian parts in which he excelled to the premieres of operas by Borodin, Musorgsky, Rimsky-Korsakov and Tchaikovsky for which he became widely renowned. And the Mariinsky loomed large in the early life of the singer's son, too. One of Igor Stravinsky's most vivid childhood memories was of being taken in 1892 to hear his father sing in the fiftieth-anniversary gala performance of Glinka's opera *Ruslan and Lyudmila*, on which occasion he caught a glimpse of Tchaikovsky in the foyer. The operas he heard at the Mariinsky made 'immediate and indelible' impressions on him, he later wrote. Their traces are left in the numerous operas, ballets and other stage works that punctuate the course of the composer's career.

Another celebrated Russian bass called Fyodor at the Imperial Opera, one Chaliapin, spoke of his predecessor's huge reputation in the 1890s, and acknowledged that he had learned much directly from Fyodor Stravinsky. Igor Fyodorovich recalled that his father had 'a beautiful voice and an amazing technique' in addition to great dramatic talent, 'a rare attribute among opera singers at that time'. He was an intelligent performer who studied carefully for each role. His meticulous preparation was undertaken at home amid his personal library of many thousands of volumes. This was his private space. He was an austere, authoritarian figure, feared by his children. For Igor and his three brothers, Roman, Yury and Gury, their father's music was only ever heard 'at a distance – from the nursery to which my brothers and I were relegated', as he wrote in the *Autobiography*. Nonetheless, music was an essential part of the fabric of the apartment. Igor had access to the unequalled resources of his father's library and gained great pleasure from sight-reading through opera scores at the piano, a skill he claimed he inherited from his mother, who was also a very good amateur musician.

The apartment on Kryukov Canal must have been a crowded place. In addition to the family of six, there was also – as was typical for a well-to-do bourgeois home of the age – the resident manservant, Semyon Ivanovich Sokolov, a Finnish cook, and, from time to time, various wet nurses and maids. And then there was Bertha Essert, the German nurse or *nyanya*, who had joined the household the year before Igor's birth and whom he came to love as a second mother. She remained devoted to two generations of the Stravinsky family, taking care not only of Fyodor's children but later of Igor's too. She died in Morges, Switzerland, in 1917, and her passing affected Stravinsky more deeply than the later loss of his own mother. He mourned for several weeks following Bertha's death.

Anna Kirillovna brought up her children in a strict atmosphere. Stravinsky much later described his childhood using such words as 'unhappy' and 'lonely'; his mother, he claimed, 'delighted' in tormenting him. Yet, though stern, Anna was not without love. She worried obsessively over the health of her children, and with good reason. Both Igor and Yury suffered bouts of tuberculosis, and while Igor's own memoirs make little of the death in 1897 of his eldest brother, Roman (he considered that his parents displayed unfair favouritism towards their first-born), it clearly affected Anna and Fyodor deeply. Neither showed their emotions openly, but Fyodor's private notebooks and Anna's letters betray two parents deeply traumatized by the loss of their son. Within five years Fyodor was also dead, from cancer. At the latter end of Igor Stravinsky's life, he recounted the details to Robert Craft. Strikingly, he records the theatricality of the rituals surrounding the death rather than his feelings about it. The Stravinsky family expressed their grief in private. 'Mournings were solemn and strict in Russia, and Gaelic-type wakes were unknown. We went home, each of us to his own room, to cry alone.'[1] But the passing of Stravinsky's father left a deeply engrained impression. Always avoiding the direct expression of grief or emotion, Stravinsky would repeat across his life this particular 'alienated theatrical experience of death' in the form of litanies that appeared in so many of his works, not least in the many musical tributes he produced to lost friends, from Debussy to Dylan Thomas.[2] One might even take a step further and suggest that the distance and restraint that were so much a part of Stravinsky's early experiences of both life and death became the defining characteristics of all his music.

Stravinsky's early education centred on the family home and was entrusted to a series of governesses. He entered school only at the age of eleven, where his academic record was undistinguished. Nonetheless, by one means or another he managed to gain admission to St Petersburg University to study law (as his father had done in Kiev), which was a common route for the upper middle classes to take towards a future safe career in the civil service. But it was clear from a relatively early age that his interests lay elsewhere, even if serious musical study was not enthusiastically encouraged by his parents. He would spend much time improvising at the piano, an activity that he later claimed was important because

Igor Stravinsky with his youngest brother, Gury, St Petersburg, *c.* 1899.

'it sowed the seed of musical ideas.' This practice continued down his working life: the piano remained Stravinsky's compositional 'workshop' and on the rare occasions he would pose at work for a photographer he was usually seated at the piano. He first took piano lessons from a young product of the Petersburg Conservatoire named Alexandra Snetkova. She was replaced in due course by Leokadiya Kashperova, a distinguished pupil of Anton Rubenstein, through whom Stravinsky gained experience and understanding of both the German and Russian pianistic repertoires. He is rather hard on her in his autobiography, but he does have the grace to acknowledge that she was an excellent musician who gave new impetus to his playing and to the development of his technique. When in the 1920s Stravinsky set about reinventing himself as a concert pianist so that he could play the solo part in his own Concerto, Kashperova must still have been looking over his shoulder as he worked intensively on the exercises in finger dexterity that formed the basis of his daily practice regime.

The winter for Stravinsky meant St Petersburg, the summer the Russian countryside. Petersburg was full of sights and sounds that stayed with him until late in life, when he recalled his early years (with varying degrees of reliability) to Craft. He remembers the sound of the fife-and-drum Marine band drifting into the nursery from the nearby barracks. He remembers that 'the whole city crackled' with the sounds of the iron-hooped wheels of horse-drawn carriages on the cobbled streets. He recalls with affection a solitary street accordion player and a café balalaika orchestra. And he remembers especially vividly the cries of the street vendors – the '*halaat, halaat*' of the Tartars, the calls in Russian of ice-cream sellers and of the knife-grinder – memories on which he was to draw in the opening tableau of *Petrushka*. 'The loudest diurnal noises of the city were the cannonade of bells from the Nikolsky Cathedral', situated just a few hundred metres away from the Kryukov Canal apartment. These were just one distinctive set of church bells, bells that were a defining feature not just of Petersburg but of the Russian landscape more generally. They resounded across the Russian music with which Stravinsky grew up, from Musorgsky's coronation of Boris Godunov to Tchaikovsky's marking of the victory over Napoleon at Borodino, and everywhere in Rimsky-Korsakov. Celebratory bells are invoked at the end of *The Firebird*; bells toll death at the end of the *Requiem Canticles*: Russian bells seem to ring out across all Stravinsky's music.

Of the built environment of Petersburg Stravinsky recalls with affection the Bourse, the Smolny Cathedral cloister, the Alexandrinsky Theatre, the Winter Palace, the Admiralty and, above all, the Mariinsky Theatre. He remembers the city's many squares, in one of which he saw his first 'Petrushka' puppet play. Petersburg was, for Stravinsky, an ochre city (like Rome), whose Italianate buildings were 'not merely by imitation but by the direct work of such architects as Quarenghi and Rastrelli'. But Italy it was not. Nor was it ancient, dark Rus'. It was a European Russia. It was a modern city of enlightenment, conjured out of barren marshland by Peter the Great at the beginning of the eighteenth century as his new imperial capital. In fact, as Orlando Figes reads it, Petersburg was more than a city: it was 'a vast, almost utopian project of cultural engineering to reconstruct the Russian as a European man'. And it was built 'as a work of art' or rather, as early European visitors experienced it, as a theatre in which the buildings were its sets and the people its actors.[3] The layout was borrowed from the canal cities of Amsterdam and Venice, the architectural style was copied from the grandest models found in England, France, Holland and Italy. And yet, 'underneath the surface of this European dream world the old Russia still showed through': 'the European Russian was a "European" on the public stage and a "Russian" in those moments of his private life when, without even thinking, he did things in a way that only Russians did'.[4] Stravinsky would spend much of his later life 'acting' the European, adopting European habits and fashions, borrowing European culture and music. From the moment of his first success in Paris, he publicly derided Petersburg as small and provincial, quickly distancing himself from the city of his upbringing. Yet in private he remained Russian through and through. In 1962, on returning to Russia for the first time in almost half a century, he declared to the daily newspaper *Komsomol'skaya pravda*: 'I've spoken Russian all my life, I think in Russian, my way of expressing myself [*slog*] is Russian. Perhaps this is not immediately apparent in my music, but it is latent there, a part of its hidden nature.'[5] He was a true son of Petersburg, but it was only as an old man that he was finally prepared to acknowledge that the city was 'dearer to my heart than any other city in the world', and that that city had had a profound influence on the man and artist he later became.

'Striving to make themselves at home with foreigners, they had become foreigners at home.'[6] While foreignness had always been central to the make-up of Petersburg, a place where Russia was concealed, it was in the countryside that a more 'authentic' Russia

Mariinsky Theatre, St Petersburg.

was to be encountered. Increasingly during the nineteenth century, following the lead of the aristocrats, the upper middle classes acquired or rented summer homes in the country. They would retreat from the city to a *dacha* in a forest or by the sea to live a simpler life, closer to nature and to the habits of rural folk. This was important to Stravinsky. It is with the memory of summer in the country that his autobiography begins: 'I can see it now. An enormous peasant seated on the stump of a tree. The sharp resinous tang of fresh-cut wood in my nostrils. The peasant simply clad in a short red shirt.' Musical recollections are foremost. Stravinsky remembers this peasant's noisy tongue clicking, his singing of a song in rapid tempo composed of just two meaningless syllables, and the way he accompanied himself with the sound of armpit farts, much to the little Igor's amusement. He remembers the unison singing of the women of the neighbouring village as they made their way home from a day's work, and more especially the praise he received for being able to imitate it accurately. With a heavy dose of hindsight, he claims in the autobiography that this marked 'the dawn of my consciousness of myself in the role of a musician'. This is highly unlikely, given that Stravinsky would have been barely two years old at the time. Yet even in his conversations with Craft in the late 1950s he again recounts the story of the countrywomen and is still able to sing the melody of their song.[7]

Except when travelling in Germany, the Stravinskys spent the long summers of the 1890s in the various country dwellings of wealthy relatives. The remote estate at Pavlovka in the Samara district (1,500 kilometres southeast of St Petersburg) belonged to Stravinsky's mother's sister Sof'ya and her husband Alexander Yelachich. Stravinsky was very fond of his Uncle Alya, a high-ranking Petersburg civil servant, but a liberal man with whom Stravinsky would discuss current politics as well as music. It was here in 1903 that he would begin the composition of his first major work, the Piano Sonata in F-sharp minor, in the shadow of

Tchaikovsky (the 'hero of my childhood'), Glazunov and Skryabin. Yekaterina, another of Anna's sisters who was married to Alexander Yelachich's brother Nikolay (who died in 1877), owned a large estate at Pechisky in western Ukraine. Stravinsky's memories of Pechisky were not, on the whole, happy ones. He despised his aunt – 'an orgulous and despotic woman who never managed to show me any kindness' – and it was there that Roman died and was buried. Nonetheless, Stravinsky does recall some aspects of rural life with delight – the fairs in nearby towns, the bright peasant costumes, music and dancing contests, all of which he was later to incorporate into *Petrushka*.

But the place that would retain the deepest affection in Stravinsky's heart was the village of Ustilug (Ustyluh), located amid the forests and wheatfields of the Volhniya region in western Ukraine, just a few kilometres from today's border with Poland. He first visited it with his family in 1890. It was the summer home of Dr Gavriil Nosenko, husband of Stravinsky's aunt Maria (who had died in 1882), and his two daughters, Lyudmila and Yekaterina. From his earliest hours together with Yekaterina, known as Katya and later as Catherine,

> we both seemed to realize that we would one day marry – or
> so we told each other later. Perhaps we were always more like
> brother and sister. I was a deeply lonely child and I wanted
> a sister of my own. Catherine . . . came into my life as a kind
> of long-wanted sister . . . We were from then until her death
> extremely close, and closer than lovers sometimes are, for mere
> lovers may be strangers though they live and love together all
> their lives.

It is a touching but also telling account of their relationship, written with the benefit of an old man's hindsight some twenty years after Catherine's death. They were indeed married, in early

1906 in the Church of the Annunciation at Novaya Derevnya, to the north of St Petersburg. Parallel-cousin marriage was forbidden in Russia, so the ceremony had to be performed in secret. (Illicit relationships were to be a recurring motif of Stravinsky's life.) Like a sister, Catherine would remain in absolute lifelong devotion to her husband, despite his many extra-marital misdemeanours, despite his temper, despite his emotional and financial neglect of her. Her faith in what she saw as her husband's divine creative talent remained unshaken throughout their married life together. As for Stravinsky, his philandering notwithstanding, he always maintained that 'I loved her from the moment I first saw her and I have always loved her.' Her framed photograph adorned his studio until his last days.

The early years of their marriage were spent living with Stravinsky's mother and his youngest brother, Gury, at the apartment on Kryukov Canal, where their first two children were born: Fyodor (1907), known as Fedik and later Theodore, and Lyudmila (1908), known as Mika or Mikushka. In 1909 they moved into a separate rented apartment just a couple of hundred metres away on the Angliyskiy Prospekt. But their spiritual home remained at Ustilug, where they would retreat each summer, and where Stravinsky would find the peace of mind (if not always the peace and quiet amid children and relatives) to compose. At first they stayed in the Nosenko family house, but in the late summer of 1908 they moved into their own new summer house, which had been built on the estate to Stravinsky's own design just a stone's throw from another new house being erected for Catherine's sister and brother-in-law, Grigory Belyankin, and their children. It was in this rural Russian idyll that Stravinsky would find the inspiration in 1911 to begin writing a work that would shock the artistic world with its violent representation of scenes of pagan Russia, and which anticipated the cataclysmic world events that prevented him after 1914 from ever returning to his beloved house again.

Stravinsky had entered St Petersburg University in the autumn of 1901. His legal studies were not, however, at the forefront of his mind. In November of that year he began taking private lessons in harmony and counterpoint with, first Fyodor Akimenko, then Vasily Kalafaty, both of whom were recent graduates of the classes of Nikolay Rimsky-Korsakov, professor of theory, composition and orchestration at the St Petersburg Conservatoire. It transpired that Rimsky-Korsakov's youngest son, Vladimir, was a fellow law student. Stravinsky befriended him, along with his brother Andrey, and managed to obtain an invitation to stay with the Rimsky-Korsakov family during the summer of 1902, while they were visiting Heidelberg. (Stravinsky's own family was spending a part of the summer nearby, where his dying father – a longstanding acquaintance of Rimsky-Korsakov *père* – was receiving medical treatment.) Stravinsky was already composing 'short piano pieces, "andantes", "melodies", and so forth', and he took a selection to show the great Russian composer. Of these, only two have survived. An undistinguished scherzo for piano is unlikely to have impressed Rimsky, assuming the twenty-year-old even showed it to him; but a Rimskian setting of Pushkin's *Tucha* (The Storm Cloud), of which Rimsky had himself made a version, piqued the senior composer's interest. Rimsky encouraged Stravinsky to continue with his counterpoint lessons and agreed to advise him from time to time. He also had enough confidence in the young man to give him orchestration projects to work on, including that of his latest opera *The Legend of the Invisible City of Kitezh*. This was the leg-up Stravinsky needed. He had been given an entrée into a significant and influential Petersburg artistic circle, the consequence of which was a rapid growth in his musical experience and ambition.

Stravinsky and his university friends, along with Rimsky-Korsakov and his conservatoire pupils, attended the Russian Symphony Concerts, which had been founded by the music publisher Mitrofan Belyayev in the 1880s in order to promote

Igor and Catherine Stravinsky with Nikolay Rimsky-Korsakov, his daughter Nadezhda and her fiancé Maximilian Steinberg, Zagorodnïy Prospekt, St Petersburg, 1908.

Russian composers. He also went to the concerts of the venerable Russian Musical Society, and to the orchestral concert series organized by the conductor and Liszt pupil Alexander Siloti, at which recent music from western Europe was programmed. Much to the conservative Rimsky's disapproval, he also periodically attended and performed at the Evenings of Contemporary Music, a somewhat chaotic series of chamber concerts, which, among other things, imported new music from abroad and gave Stravinsky his first taste of Debussy. Established as an alternative to the likes of the Russian Symphony Concerts, the Evenings attracted a circle of bourgeois young aesthetes who were, at the same time, involved with a radical journal called *Mir iskusstva* (The World of Art), edited by one Sergey Diaghilev. Most important of all for Stravinsky at this stage in his life, he frequented the lively Wednesday evening soirées at the Rimsky-Korsakov apartment on Zagorodnïy Prospekt, where all manner of prominent Petersburgers met to play music and argue into the early hours of the morning. His first visit, in fact, was on Rimsky's 59th birthday, on which occasion Stravinsky's witty piano improvisations certainly impressed the distinguished select company, which included the composer Glazunov, and the influential critics Stasov and Ossovsky. This inexperienced young musician clearly already had the self-assurance to recognize that, in order to progress in the world, he needed to move among the right people. It was an instinct that would never desert him, taking him in the course of his future life from the most chic Paris salons to dinner at the White House. It was also at these Zagorodnïy gatherings that the earliest performances of Stravinsky's own music took place. The first was a cantata (presumed lost) for choir and piano written to celebrate Rimsky-Korsakov's sixtieth birthday. '*Neduren*', 'not bad', was Rimsky's verdict. The Piano Sonata, which he had begun at Pavlovka and whose composition was suspended to write the cantata, was premiered by his friend Nikolay Richter in 1905 and duly received approval from the Rimsky circle. After that Stravinsky set to work on his first large-canvas work, the four-movement Symphony in E-flat, which he was to ordain his 'Opus 1'.

The bulk of the symphony was composed in short score at Ustilug in the summer of 1905. But this was by no means the finished product. It would not in fact receive its first full public performance until 1908. From the autumn of 1905 Stravinsky began taking weekly private lessons in composition and orchestration from Rimsky-Korsakov, their first major project together being the symphony. It is clear that Rimsky had a strong hand in guiding Stravinsky through the orchestration and substantial revision of the work – indeed, the physical traces of the teacher's hand can be witnessed in the many pencil annotations on the manuscript.[8] It is an apprentice work that reveals Stravinsky's deep familiarity with the Russian symphonists – much direct borrowing from Glazunov, as well as from Borodin, Taneyev, Tchaikovsky and Rimsky himself – in addition to strong allusions to other composers with whose music he was familiar, including Sibelius and Wagner.

It even incorporated folk tunes, just as his venerable forebears had done – the so-called *Moguchaya kuchka* or 'Mighty Handful'. As Richard Taruskin puts it, Stravinsky's Opus 'was an oath of fealty' to those figures.'[9]

Stravinsky's compositional confidence was growing fast, though there was still little indication of the original imagination that would emerge in just a few years. There were three Pushkin songs called *The Faun and the Shepherdess*, begun at the same time as the symphony, which betray, among other things, the passion for Wagner he had harboured since his early teens. There were two settings of his Petersburg contemporary Sergey Gorodetsky, which offer the first instance of Stravinsky imitating the clamour of tolling bells. And there were two showy orchestral scherzos. The *Scherzo fantastique* was based on a programme about bees derived from Maeterlinck, but which Stravinsky later attempted to suppress in part through fear of comparison with another much-loved piece about bees by his teacher. In any case, both the *Scherzo* and *Fireworks* demonstrate just how indebted Stravinsky was to Rimsky-Korsakov, not only in their dazzling orchestration but in the adept way they deploy the magical whole-tone, octatonic and chromatic harmonies found in Rimsky's operas. *Fireworks* was written as a wedding present for Rimsky's daughter Nadezhda, and no doubt he had hoped that the work would please his teacher. It was not to be. Rimsky-Korsakov died on 8 June 1908 (os) before the manuscript could reach him. Stravinsky was devastated. It was for him the loss of a second father.

On 24 January 1909 Siloti conducted the premiere of the *Scherzo fantastique*. In the audience was Diaghilev. Moving in the same circles, he and Stravinsky would have had several previous opportunities to meet, but it is unlikely that they had ever exchanged words. 'Of course I knew who he was', recalled Stravinsky, 'everyone did'. On another occasion Diaghilev heard *Fireworks*, which also made a great impression on him. 'It is new

and original, with a tonal quality that should surprise the public',
he told his manager, Sergey Grigoriev. Diaghilev sent Stravinsky
his card, asking Stravinsky to call on him. It was the beginning
of a partnership – creative, passionate, turbulent – that would
last until Diaghilev's death twenty years later, and which would
change not only the course of Stravinsky's career but the face of
twentieth-century art for good.

2

Russian Ballets

Gare du Nord, June 1910. Igor Stravinsky arrives in Paris from Ustilug in a state of high excitement. Though he has never set foot in the city before, he feels he already knows it well, thanks to his cosmopolitan upbringing in St Petersburg. The second *saison russe* is well under way. The enthusiasm in Paris for this parade of Russian exoticism proves undiminished. And the word about town is that the new work *The Firebird* is the must-see of the year. The company's impresario, Sergey Diaghilev, has been hard at work stirring up a frenzy about his latest protégé, the boy genius of Russian music. 'Mark him well,' Diaghilev tells his dancers in rehearsal, 'he is a man on the eve of celebrity!' And so, on 25 June in the glamorous surroundings of the Opéra, seated in Diaghilev's box amid the richest and most famous of high Paris society, Stravinsky awaits the rise of the curtain. The golden designs of Alexander Golovin and Léon Bakst, the dancing of Tamara Karsavina and Mikhail Fokine in Fokine's alluring choreography, and the magical sounds produced by Stravinsky's orchestra send the audience wild. Stravinsky and his collaborators are called back to the stage many times at the end. It all rather goes to Stravinsky's head. His friends observe him in raptures over the French. 'Only here do you find real taste and art!' he cries. Just as Diaghilev predicts, Stravinsky is the name on everyone's lips, and this 28-year-old's life is changed forever. His destiny, he decides, now lies in France, and he hurries back to Ustilug to collect Catherine and the children so that they too can come to Paris to witness his success.

It is true that *The Firebird* made Stravinsky, though in retrospect it can just as well be argued that Stravinsky made *The Firebird*. Despite its collective origins, Stravinsky was soon claiming sole authorship of the work by turning the ballet into an orchestral suite. As an émigré in America in the 1940s he came to be defined in public largely by this one work, which he conducted frequently in order to make a living at a time when the flow of royalties from occupied Europe had virtually dried up. He would be stopped in the street in Hollywood and asked, much to his exasperation, 'Excuse me, aren't you the composer of *The Firebird*?' He recalls with some amusement a man in an American railway dining car addressing him as 'Mr Fireberg'. Even in death he and his first ballet score were inseparable: the 'Register of Friends Who Called' at Frank E. Campbell's New York funeral parlour in April 1971 includes an anonymous 'Firebird Lover'. But it could so easily have been otherwise. Stravinsky had been a latecomer to the *Firebird* project. Diaghilev only turned to this 'promising beginner' out of desperation after a roster of senior Petersburg composers had let him down or had rejected his approaches: Tcherepnin and Lyadov certainly, perhaps also Glazunov and Sokolov. And by then the scenario had already been worked out in detail, the production designs were under way, and Stravinsky was simply required to slot in as best he could and do as he was told.

The origins of *The Firebird* are, inevitably, wrapped up with the ambitions and complex personality of Diaghilev. Born into the minor nobility in 1872, Diaghilev's upbringing – like Stravinsky's – was cosmopolitan and musical. Predictably, at the age of eighteen, he was sent to St Petersburg University to enrol on a law course to prepare him for entry into the civil service. But, as with his younger compatriot, his passions lay elsewhere. He was an enthusiastic composer who had come under the spell of Wagner. In 1894 he decided to present a portfolio of his compositions to Rimsky-Korsakov, but Rimsky could see no merit in them at all. 'History will show which of us was the greater!' Diaghilev is alleged to have shouted at Rimsky. But this absolute rejection by St Petersburg's most important composer was a devastating blow. Having set all his hopes on a life in music, his future now seemed bleak. To console himself he set about collecting art, initially by Russians, with the intention of acquiring impressive adornments for his new apartment on Liteynïy Prospekt. Rapidly he reinvented himself as an art historian, critic and promoter, travelling the continent in search of works by progressive European and American artists. In a perceptive act of self-analysis, he recognized that this was where his destiny lay, as he wrote to his stepmother in October 1895:

> First of all I am a great charlatan, although one with flair; second I'm a great charmer; third I've great nerve; fourth I'm a man with a great deal of logic and few principles; and fifth, I think I lack talent; but if you like, I think I've found my real calling – patronage of the arts. Everything has been given me but money – *mais ça viendra*.[1]

Recalling Diaghilev in 1953, Stravinsky summed up his extraordinary ability to motivate others as like that of the Russian *barin* (*grand seigneur*):

> It is only by understanding the nature of a cultured *barin* such as used to exist in Russia (a nature generous, strong, and capricious; with intense will, a rich sense of contrasts, and deep ancestral roots) that we can explain the character and originality of Diaghilev's creations, so different from the average artistic enterprises . . . Born to command, he knew how to make people obey him by sheer prestige and authority, without recourse to violence. He displayed characteristics of

the enlightened despot, of the natural leader who knows how to drive the most unyielding elements, at times using persuasion, at others, charm . . . Working with him . . . meant working solely for the great cause of art.[2]

Diaghilev's first exhibition opened in St Petersburg in January 1897. Having proved his skills as an organizer, he was hungry to undertake more. He had strong views on what the Russian art of the future should be, and he was already attacking in print the work of the predominant realistic and utilitarian artistic movement of the day, the so-called *peredvizhniki* ('itinerants'). He had plans to produce a periodical in which he would present reproductions of paintings and write polemical pieces, and which would act as an outlet for a movement that promoted a neo-nationalist Russian art that transcended both artistic and national boundaries. 'Art for art's sake' was to be its rallying cry, though that turned out to be a crude slogan. The inaugural issue of *Mir iskusstva* appeared in October 1898 (dated January 1899); its first lengthy editorial went straight on the attack against those who had accused the embryonic movement of decadence. The new generation of artists was dedicated to 'the exaltation and glorification of individualism in art', to the freedom of individual expression, to pleasure and beauty, and at the same time to making a genuinely Russian national art.[3]

Though Diaghilev was the primary moving force and editor-in-chief of *Mir iskusstva*, it was from the start a collective enterprise. The central organizing and editorial committee was made up of men who had been together variously since their school and student days, well-to-do aesthetes who would spend their time in their self-styled 'Nevsky Pickwickians' club discussing art and philosophy, and attending opera and ballet. They included the artist and writer Alexander Benois, Diaghilev's aristocratic cousin and sometime lover Dmitry Filosofov ('Dima'), the co-founder of the Evenings of Contemporary Music and future ghostwriter of Stravinsky's autobiography, Walter Nouvel, and the artist Léon Bakst. These men contributed items to the journal and made works for their exhibitions. Swiftly *Mir iskusstva* established a reputation as the most progressive and fashionable force in Petersburg. Yet it is striking that in turning their faces to the future the *miriskusniki* adopted a retrospective stance. They looked back beyond the nineteenth century in order to restore the (aristocratic) values of an earlier age. In the highly stylized art of Benois and Bakst, for instance, the neoclassical architecture of St Petersburg was often a source of inspiration. Progressive aesthetic theories were presented in the journal in a typeface derived from an eighteenth-century French model. Russian folk art and traditions were embraced, as if they too were representative of a 'purer' classical past. If aspects of this carry uncanny pre-echoes of Stravinsky's later aesthetic, self-consciously constructing a pan-European modernist music that looked back to much earlier models, then this only goes to alert one to the formative influence the key players in the *Mir iskusstva* movement had on the young composer. For all their radical pronouncements, *Mir iskusstva* and Stravinsky alike essentially adopted a conservative attitude: not art as a mirror to the world, not art as politics; just art for art's sake.

Yet not even the *miriskusniki*, however, could remain aloof from unfolding events. The death of the autocratic Tsar Alexander III in 1894 had raised the hopes of liberals for greater representation of the people, but his son and successor, Nicholas II, made few meaningful concessions. Discontent and violence were growing all around. A disastrous war with Japan and poor harvests, along with the increasing influence of revolutionaries, led to serious unrest amid workers and students. Peasants attacked landowners' estates, industrial workers staged strikes and students rebelled. On Sunday 9 January 1905 (os) a group of workers marched peacefully

Cover of *Mir iskusstva* by Yelena Polenova (vol. II, 1899).

on the Winter Palace in St Petersburg to present a petition to the Tsar, but they were shot down in cold blood. News of the Bloody Sunday massacre spread quickly. Petersburg was soon crippled by a general strike, and even the military revolted, most famously in the mutiny on the battleship *Potemkin*. Nicholas eventually conceded to the formation of an elected assembly or *duma*, though in practice this did little to limit the tsar's powers. The universities were granted autonomy, but not before Rimsky-Korsakov had been dismissed from his position at the Conservatoire for publicly siding with students in their demand for an end to state censorship of the arts. Even Stravinsky, who was more disturbed than riled by the violent events taking place around him, was arrested and detained when he inadvertently became caught up in a demonstration. Diaghilev supported the striking dancers at the Imperial Theatre. Like Stravinsky, he was on the side of change, but the primary emotions felt by all those on the margins of these events were fear and uncertainty.

Given the turbulent state of St Petersburg, Diaghilev looked to promote Russian culture abroad. In any case, the success of his early artistic ventures served to fan the flames of his driving ambition. Russian folk art had been received enthusiastically at the Exposition Universelle in Paris in 1900, which Diaghilev had attended. He now grasped the opportunity to sow neo-nationalist Russian art on this fertile Paris soil and, with Benois and Bakst, mounted a well-received Russian exhibition at the 1906 Paris Salon d'Automne. But could its success be repeated? Never one to be daunted by the size of a project, Diaghilev next devised a series of concerts for the Paris Opéra in 1907, which imported Rimsky-Korsakov to conduct his own music and Chaliapin to sing an aria from Borodin's *Prince Igor*. Full-scale opera followed in 1908, a staged performance of *Boris Godunov* with Chaliapin in the title role. A team of designers including Benois and Golovin made sumptuous sets and costumes from all manner of fabrics and objects collected from across Russia, echoing the interest in folk arts and crafts that had been represented in even the earliest issues of *Mir iskusstva*. The resulting production, though lavish, was far from authentic: 'it was one big multi-ethnic, ahistorical hotchpotch of the most eye-catching exotica the Russian empire could offer.'[4] It was nonetheless an overwhelming success. It gave French audiences thirsty for a primitive and exotic Russia exactly what they desired – a desire, indeed, that Diaghilev had largely been responsible for cultivating. And so the stage was set for the launch in 1909 of Diaghilev's most ambitious project yet, an enterprise that was, in Stravinsky's words, 'able to breathe new life into the ballet, to change its form, to coordinate the different elements of which it was composed, to make it completely homogeneous, and to raise it to the highest degree of art'. Its influence would reach across the world.

The spectacular first *saison russe* of opera and ballet productions opened at the Théâtre du Châtelet on 19 May 1909. Once again, members of the Imperial Theatres – dancers, singers, musicians, stage crew – were all shipped to Paris for the summer to present no fewer than eight works in three different programmes. Fokine devised the choreography while the designs were shared among Bakst, Benois, Golovin, Nicholas Roerich (Nikolay Rerikh) and others. The undoubted stars of the shows, for which *le tout-Paris* had been clamouring, were the dancers: Fokine himself, Anna Pavlova (whose portrait was displayed on posters all over Paris), Tamara Karsavina and Vaslav Nijinsky, this last hyped up by Diaghilev as 'the new Vestris', the *dieu de la danse* of late eighteenth-century Paris. And in the midst of all this was *Les Sylphides*, a non-narrative ballet set to a potpourri of music by Chopin, first seen (as *Chopiniana*) in St Petersburg in 1907 and to which a nocturne and waltz had now been added, newly orchestrated by Stravinsky. These were his audition pieces for Diaghilev. Evidently the great impresario was pleased with the result. Within months he had sent a telegram to Ustilug to enquire of Stravinsky if, in principle, he would be prepared to write a score for a ballet being prepared for the 1910 Paris season. Excitedly Stravinsky began sketching, even though he did not receive the official commission until the end of the year.

Ballet in Paris had become grey, routine and predictable. The colours and rhythms of the first Russian season had opened the eyes and ears of Paris society to a very different, vibrant, virile art form. Diaghilev wanted to capitalize on this by creating something entirely new. The *miriskusniki* – Benois most especially – had long admired ballet, not least for the fact that its synthesis of music, dance, drama and design offered the possibility for the realization of the Wagnerian notion of *Gesamtkunstwerk* ('total work of art'), which they so admired. In 1907 Benois, Fokine and Nijinsky had come together for the first time to mount a new work at the Mariinsky, *Le Pavillon d'Armide*, to a story by Gautier with music by Tcherepnin, which was remounted for the 1909 *saison russe*. Now, as Diaghilev wrote to Lyadov:

> I need a *ballet*, and a *Russian* one – the *first* Russian ballet, for there is no such thing as yet. There is Russian opera, Russian symphony, Russian song, Russian dance, Russian rhythm – but no Russian ballet.

And so the *Zhar-ptitsa* or *Firebird* project was conceived, and constructed from various fairy tales found in a variety of sources, principally the influential collections made in the nineteenth century by folklorist Alexander Afanas'yev. The eventual scenario telling of a magical kingdom and creatures, a beautiful princess and a heroic prince had all the exotic Russian colour necessary to thrill Paris once more. It fitted perfectly what Benois called a 'mysterium of Russia' for 'export to the West'. It was entirely authentic and yet, at the same time, an illusion, a nostalgic invention of a folk past.

Stravinsky worked at a prodigious rate, completing the fully orchestrated score within six months. It is often quipped that *The Firebird* is the finest score Rimsky-Korsakov never wrote. Certainly in the virtuosity of its orchestration it stands proudly alongside the work of Stravinsky's late teacher. The opulence of the ballet's sets and costumes was more than matched by the richness and variety of his use of the large orchestra. There are many striking effects throughout. Stravinsky's own favourite was the glissando of string harmonics near the beginning, which he claims astonished even Richard Strauss. The score has an animated rhythmic language which, while derived from the practices of his Russian forebears, anticipates in places the rhythmic innovations of his succeeding works, not least in the well-known 'Infernal dance', as well as in the repeating rhythmic layers and exotic harmonies of the '*carillon féerique*', the 'Magical Carillon, Appearance of Kashchey's Monster-Guardians, and Capture of Ivan-Tsarevich'. Elsewhere, there are simple folk-like melodies, notably for Ivan, in the manner of Rimsky. But perhaps its greatest achievement is its drama. Stravinsky worked closely with Fokine at every stage and, as a result, scenario, choreography and design are bound tightly together by the music. Indeed, it was the integrated nature of the ballet that so impressed many of the French reviewers of the premiere performances: 'the most exquisite marvel of equilibrium that we have ever imagined between sounds, movements and forms'.[5] Recurring musical motifs were deployed in an almost operatic manner (after Wagner) to represent characters and situations. Harmonies, too, as in Rimsky's operas, were used to delineate characters: the fantastical world of Kashchey and the firebird were associated with exotic harmonies – particularly the eight-note diminished or octatonic scale, known to Stravinsky as the Rimsky-Korsakov scale – while the human characters such as the princess were, in the main, diatonic.

In sum, *The Firebird* is Stravinsky's journeyman work. His complete ownership of the techniques of so much Russian music that preceded it, sustained over such a large scale, is in itself highly impressive for a relatively inexperienced composer. While ultimately the score lacked any truly great originality, in its flair it asserted, in the words of one of Stravinsky's earliest Soviet supporters, 'active sovereignty over lesson and precept' (meaning the conservative tendencies of the Rimsky school).[6] But what *The Firebird* demonstrated beyond doubt was Stravinsky's instinct for the role music could play in the theatre – perhaps not so surprising for one who had grown up with the Mariinsky as his second home. In transferring the techniques of opera to ballet, the contribution of Stravinsky to the reinvention of dance for the twentieth century cannot be underestimated.

The success of *The Firebird* thrust Stravinsky instantly into the wealthiest and most influential circles in Paris. Smitten, he chose to remain in France rather than return to Russia, spending the summer with his family at a seaside hotel in La Baule, Brittany. Then, in September, the family moved to Lausanne, Switzerland, where Catherine gave birth to their third child, Svyatoslav, known as Svetik (and who, in the 1930s, adopted the old Polish family name Soulima as his professional name). Stravinsky's primary objective was to press on with composing his next major project, another ballet for the following Paris season of Diaghilev's company, which had now been re-established in its own right as a year-round operation under the name of the Ballets Russes. The idea for the work, or so Stravinsky claimed, had come to him in a vision, though it is more than likely that the initial impetus came from Roerich, a Russian folklorist and member of the Diaghilev circle since 1904, to whom Stravinsky had turned for assistance. It was to be called 'The Great Sacrifice'. But in Switzerland the idea was temporarily shelved and instead he began work on 'a sort of *Konzertstück*', as he called it in the *Autobiography*, for piano and orchestra, which he imagined as 'a distant picture of a puppet, suddenly endowed with life, exasperating the patience of the orchestra with diabolical cascades of arpeggios'. Soon afterwards Diaghilev visited Stravinsky in Switzerland and was astonished by what he heard. Diaghilev instantly wanted it to be turned into a ballet and convinced Stravinsky to contact Benois, who had long been fascinated by old Russian puppet theatres. He seemed the perfect person to help develop Stravinsky's idea. But Benois took months to respond to Stravinsky's overtures, so he just continued composing. Unlike *The Firebird*, then, much of the music of *Petrushka* (as it became) was already written before a detailed scenario emerged, and when that finally did appear, Stravinsky had a strong hand in shaping it along with the choreography. This helped liberate Stravinsky's compositional imagination. Thus, while *The Firebird* represented the culmination of an essentially nineteenth-century Russian style, *Petrushka* marks the beginning of Stravinsky as a modernist with an emerging musical identity all his own. It is an extraordinary leap forward.

The scenario reimagines a multicoloured Russian past, the action taking place in the 1830s at the Shrovetide fair in Admiralty Square, St Petersburg. In the words of the original version of the score, the opening tableau presents a bustling scene:

> A sunny winter's day . . . a large booth with a balcony . . .
> a table with an enormous samovar . . . the little theatre of
> the Charlatan . . . sweetmeat stalls and a showman of optical
> illusions . . . a roundabout with gentlefolk, troupes of drunkards
> . . . children . . .

Benois reached back deep into the nineteenth century for his source material. Stravinsky demonstrated a parallel concern for authenticity in his use of a broad range of folk and popular melodies. Though the borrowed materials were by no means exclusively Russian (a popular French chansonette, Joseph Lanner waltzes, and so on), they would have been circulating widely in Russia at the time. Springing up directly from the street, as it were, the music would have had a rough immediacy that appealed to the Paris enthusiasts – 'childlike and untamed' Debussy called the music – even while early Russian audiences thought it just a tasteless collage of *trukha* (rubbish).

The first tableau, like the later sequence of dances, beguiles with its glittering orchestral colour and apparent *joie de vivre*, articulating a nostalgic desire to return to the lost world of Benois' and Stravinsky's childhood. The music of the opening tableau cuts in an almost cinematic manner from a general view

Igor Stravinsky
with Vaslav
Nijinsky in the
costume of
Petrushka, 1911.

of the milling crowd to close-ups of individuals or groups (a barker, dancers, a barrel organ player) and back again. Borrowed musical materials are fractured, reconfigured, denied their expected development. Stravinsky seems to be longing to return to a world that he knows has already been shattered, a world that is indeed only the product of his imagination. In this sense the musical fragmentation speaks presciently of the rapidly changing world in which he lived. The resulting sense of alienation is embodied in the character of the suffering Petrushka, whose part-human, part-puppet sides cannot be reconciled. This is captured in the dissonant 'Petrushka chord' with its superposition of the most distant possible triads of C and F-sharp major. Petrushka's eventual death goes unnoticed by the world around him: he is alienated from that world; he is as powerless to affect it as is the Chosen One sacrificed at the end of Stravinsky's next work, *The Rite of Spring*. In attempting to recreate a vanished Russia as authentically as possible, *Petrushka* unwittingly anticipates the tragedy that was soon to overwhelm not just Russia but the whole of Europe.

Petrushka was premiered by the Ballets Russes at the Théâtre du Chatelet on 13 June 1911, designed by Benois, choreographed by Fokine, conducted by Pierre Monteux, and danced by Karsavina as the Ballerina and Nijinsky as Petrushka. It was given a rapturous reception. Its success gave Stravinsky the confidence to push his new musical thinking still further. At the end of the season he returned to Ustilug to resume work on 'The Great Sacrifice'.

3

Portrait of a Scandal

Thursday 29 May 1913. Théâtre des Champs-Élysées, avenue Montaigne.
All fashionable Paris is here. Brand new chauffeur-driven motor
cars jostle for position with horse-drawn carriages. Aristocrats,
diplomats and the *demi-monde* throng the pavement outside the
theatre. The trappings of wealth and privilege are on ostentatious
display: aigrettes, ostrich feathers and pearls aplenty, tulle gowns,
top hats and tailcoats. Decadent French society has fallen in love
with the Ballets Russes, in whose exotic productions it finds its
glamorous counterpart. On the bill tonight are *Les Sylphides*, *Le
Spectre de la rose* and *Prince Igor*, three favourites choreographed
by Fokine from earlier seasons. And there is a palpable sense of
excitement as they await the premiere of the latest spectacle
Diaghilev has devised for them. Excitement along with a frisson
of danger. Some of them have already seen Nijinsky's other
new work of the season, *Jeux*, in the same theatre just three
weeks earlier. Debussy's subtle music and Nijinsky's awkward
choreography baffled them. They greeted it with laughter.
Rumours are now circulating about this new ballet from Nijinsky
called *Le Sacre du printemps* to a score by Stravinsky. The lush
designs and seductive costumes they so love from the Ballets
Russes have been replaced, so they understand, by shapeless
dresses and peculiar headwear. They hear whispers of unnatural
poses and violent movements. And the music is said to be nothing
but primitive banging.

A posed group of dancers in the original production of *The Rite of Spring*, against the backdrop by Nicholas Roerich, 1913.

The audience take their seats, Stravinsky among them. He sits with his wife, Catherine, in the stalls, close to the stage. Silence descends as the house lights are dimmed. The conductor, Pierre Monteux, arrives in front of the orchestra and raises his baton. Then from the pit emerge unexpected, strangled sounds: a solo bassoon, unbelievably high in its register. This is certainly not the romantic reverie of *Les Sylphides*. From the off the music appears strange. One by one, other wind instruments join in with twisted chromatic lines and dislocated melodic fragments layered one on top of another. It is the sound of 'nature renewing itself', or so Stravinsky attempts to explain in an essay published that very day. But this is already too much for the philistines in the audience. They want glamour and all they get is this ugliness – just like the austere new building they are sitting in, which they dislike intensely. They begin to mutter among themselves. Others shush them loudly. Sniggering starts as one young man tries to match the sounds of the instruments by vocalizing animal noises. And all this even before the front curtain has gone up.

The curtain rises to reveal a mysterious hill and figures grouped in circles about the stage. A powerfully dissonant chord sounds in the orchestra, repeated over and over, but with unpredictable cross accents. The dancers jerk into life almost like puppets, jumping and hopping in unison to the pulse of the repeated chord, their arms making sudden and ungainly movements. They shake and quake and tremble. An old woman with sticks, bent double, moves among them. Already predisposed to mock anything out of the ordinary, a man from the gallery calls out loudly for a doctor, to howls of laughter. A phalanx of Young Maidens moves from the back of the stage, feet turned inwards, heads inclined and resting in their hands. '*Un dentiste!*', shouts a woman. '*Deux dentistes!*', calls another. More raucous laughter ensues. 'It's the first time in 60 years that anyone has dared make a fool of me', calls out the red-faced comtesse de Pourtalès, waving her fan. She gets up noisily to leave, along with some of her companions. This is too much for the work's supporters, disgusted at such a display of ignorance from these high-society snobs. '*Taisez-vous, les garces du seizième!*' – 'Shut up, you posh bitches!' – the composer and critic Florent Schmitt spits at them. And so the jeering, cheering, laughing, whistling and cat-calling escalate, one side trying to outdo the other. A cane is brandished. An elegant lady slaps the face of a hissing young man. A punch is thrown. Stravinsky has had enough. He jumps up indignantly and storms out of the auditorium, making his way backstage.

The dancers can now no longer hear the orchestra amid the uproar in the auditorium. Diaghilev had anticipated trouble. 'Whatever happens,' he entreated the cast before the performance started, 'keep going.' So they persist. In the wings, standing on a chair, Nijinsky furiously attempts to keep the dancers together by calling out numbers. 'Sixteen, seventeen, eighteen!' he screams in Russian. He is ready to leap on to the stage in protest but Stravinsky, now at his side, knows this will only make things worse. He grabs hold of Nijinsky's coat tails to restrain him. Diaghilev, meanwhile, is calling for the house lights to be turned on and off. He hopes this might pacify the public, but it in fact just succeeds in inflaming the protesters further. While the lights are on, the police, who have been summoned, come rushing into the theatre and drag out the leading culprits. This calms things temporarily, but once the lights are dimmed again, the din recommences louder than before. Remarkably, the performance continues to its very end and, as the limp body of the sacrificial victim is raised aloft by shamans in bear skins, uproarious cheers and applause drown out the residual booing. Stravinsky and Nijinsky are called to the stage many times to take their bows and receive the adulation of the standing public.

In the days that followed, the press was as divided as the first-night audience. Baptised 'Le Massacre du printemps', the work was condemned by many: 'a strange spectacle, a laborious and puerile barbarism'; 'in the desire to make things primitive, prehistoric, he [Stravinsky] has worked to bring his music close to noise'. For some it was the rhythmically asymmetric and discordant music that offended; for others it was the ugliness of the 'epileptic convulsions' in Nijinsky's choreography. For others still, however, it marked 'the beginning of a new stage in the activity of Stravinsky . . . the man of his time and perhaps its prophet'; Stravinsky was hailed a 'genius', 'the Messiah we have been waiting for since Wagner'. There was, then, little agreement. But what the reporting of the *Rite* and its celebrated riot singularly achieved was to turn it into a spectacular *succès de scandale*. Stravinsky and his *Rite* became the talk not only of the town but of the whole musical world.

The oft-told tale of the opening night riot has become the stuff of legend. But how far are the stories to be trusted? There was undoubtedly some sort of commotion, though the details vary considerably as to its extent, and it is certainly the case that accounts of the scandal became more exaggerated as time went on. The vast majority of the press was not in fact present on the evening of 29 May but had been invited, as was the custom, to attend the open *répétition générale* the day before, along with some of the most important figures in Paris artistic life, Debussy and Ravel among them. That performance was enthusiastically received, without any hint of booing or fisticuffs. For such an audience, the newness of the *Rite* was a source of fascination. So what went wrong the following night? Since 1912, in Cocteau's cutting analysis, well-to-do 'society' had come to mistake a 'false audacity' in art for 'true audacity'; when the *really* new exploded onto the stage in the form of this wild, primitive, 'Fauvist' work, the aristocracy – such as the old countess in her tiara – revealed their true colours. In Cocteau's memorable phrase, the 'provinces [were] out-provincialized in the very heart of Paris'.[1] The conditions for a riot, however, were assured when (so the story goes) Diaghilev handed out free tickets to young radicals, aesthetes and musicians, all fervently committed to the new and opposed to the snobbery of the privileged classes. Diaghilev lit the touchpaper and then stood back to watch the fireworks that inevitably ensued. Stravinsky reports that, after the performance, Diaghilev's only comment was, 'Exactly what I wanted.' What better way to bring the new work to wide attention, and to revive flagging interest in the Ballets Russes? Whatever Stravinsky later claimed, the riot on 29 May 1913 had little to do with his music, which, for much of the performance, would probably not have been audible above the cacophony in the auditorium.

There was no repetition of the audience violence at subsequent performances. Six weeks after its French premiere, the Theatre Royal in Drury Lane received *The Rite of Spring* quietly: *The Times* noted that 'London audiences have settled down calmly to a new development of the ballet after a comparatively short acquaintance with it.' In any case, the initial shock of the new, it would seem, had had more to do with the dancing than with the music. It was Diaghilev who had developed an enthusiasm for the method of eurhythmics devised by Émile Jaques-Dalcroze, and it was Diaghilev who was determined that Nijinsky, despite his inexperience, should use these techniques in the ballet. The result was as far removed as one could imagine from the traditions of the classical ballet. In place of conventional choreography was to be found a succession of rhythmically moving groups, with the dancers adopting ritualized gestures, naturalistic shivers and bodily jerks, limbs twisted at unnatural angles. The only true solo was the final sacrifice of the Chosen One, danced by Marie Piltz. But even here the repeated gestures – in direct imitation of the music – were far from lyrical and expressive: the victim was increasingly taken over by animalistic spasms and irregular convulsions. Cocteau, again, caught the measure of it:

> The fault lies in the parallelism of music and movement, in their want of 'play', of counterpoint. We had the proof that the same chord repeated often tires the ear less than the frequent repetition of the same gesture tires the eye. Laughter was caused by a monotony, as of automata, rather than by the abruptness of the attitudes, and by the abruptness of the attitudes rather than by the polyphony.[2]

Nevertheless, in an interview published on the day of the premiere, Stravinsky expressed himself 'happy to have found in Nijinsky the ideal creative collaborator'. The press thought otherwise. 'How could such a musician have allowed himself to be won over by contagion and to transfer into his art this dancer's aesthetic?' Stung by such comments, Stravinsky later did a complete volte-face and charged Nijinsky with being unmusical, claiming that the choreography had had nothing to do with the music. Within a year the work had been reinvented as a concert piece. The first Paris concert presentation was heard in respectful silence and celebrated as an unmitigated triumph.

In subsequent years Stravinsky worked with some success to whitewash his collaborators out of the genesis of the work, laying claim to it as entirely of his own making. *The Rite of Spring*, he said, 'exists as a piece of music first and last'; 'there is no story at all and no point in looking for one'. Most extraordinary of all, late in life, he asserted, 'I am the vessel through which *Le Sacre* passed', as if it had no history, as if Musorgsky or Rimsky-Korsakov or Alexander Serov, from whose work it had sprung, had never existed. These claims are simply unsustainable. Like the previous two ballets Stravinsky had written for Diaghilev, *The Rite of Spring* was a genuinely collaborative project. Like *The Firebird* and *Petrushka*, it grew out of his involvement with former *miriskusniki*. Their ruling aesthetic had been the renewal of art through an engagement with native folk culture, and while the journal itself had ceased to exist since 1904, in many ways *The Rite of Spring* would seem to stand as the culmination of *Mir iskusstva* thinking in its authentic yet modernist representation of Russian folk life.

Stravinsky's unverifiable account of the initial idea for the *Rite* is given in the *Autobiography*. In the spring of 1910, as he was completing *The Firebird*, he claims he had a vision of 'a solemn pagan rite: sage elders, seated in a circle, watched a young girl dance herself to death. They were sacrificing her to propitiate the god of spring.' Stravinsky turned to his friend Roerich for help in fleshing out the scenario for a work still called at that time 'The Great Sacrifice'. Roerich tells a different story, namely that it was he, not Stravinsky, who first came up with the idea. It is certainly the case that he had been engaged with similar subject-matter long before Stravinsky: Roerich was a leading authority on Slavic folk art and ritual, an archaeologist, anthropologist and artist who was fascinated by a pagan, prehistoric, patriarchal Russia. He had already designed a production of dances from Borodin's *Prince Igor* for the first *saison russe* in 1909, and his artistic work possessed a primitive directness that appealed to Stravinsky. Together they worked on the details in Talashkino, an artists' colony devoted to folk art, established by Princess Maria Tenisheva, an early sponsor of *Mir iskusstva*, in the Smolensk region of Russia. The music was composed in part at Ustilug, but mainly in Clarens on the banks of Lake Geneva, now Stravinsky's principal residence on account of his family's poor health.

The scenario devised by Roerich and Stravinsky is authentic in almost every detail to pagan Russian midsummer festivals, with the exception of the final sacrifice, which is their own invention and for which there is no evidence in folk practices. It went through many versions. Stravinsky's text, published shortly before the premiere, outlines the content of the work's two parts. The first, which he here names 'The Kiss of the Earth' (later 'Adoration of the Earth'), begins with an orchestral introduction representing the 'joy of spring' by imitating a swarm of *dudki* (spring pipes), ancient Slavic games, a *khorovod* (ring dance), the procession of the Old Wise Man, and a frenzied dance (the 'Dance of the Earth'). The second part, which he names 'The Great Offering' (later 'The Sacrifice'), depicts the preparation of the chosen maiden for the sacrifice, her last 'Sacred Dance' witnessed by the Old Wise Men and her death. Stravinsky's stated aim throughout the whole work was to give the listener a sense of the closeness of the people to the earth, of the commonality of their lives with the earth, principally by means of 'lapidary rhythms'. All this comes very close to accounts of peasant practices found in the sources that Roerich would have consulted, principally those concerning the Slavic sun god Yarilo:

Belarusians hold a celebration in [Yarilo's] honour at the time of the first sowing, which falls on 27 April in Belarus. The ritual at this festival is as follows. In the evening (at twilight) a khorovod of maidens assembles in a house, and there they elect one of the maidens as Yarilo, dress her up just as they imagine Yarilo, and seat her on a white horse fastened to a pole. The other girls

wind around Yarilo in a long line and dance the khorovod . . .
It is noteworthy that, in Belarusian khorovod celebrations,
it is usually the girls, not the men (boys), who play the chief
and exclusive role.[3]

Such authenticity of detail extended beyond the scenario to Roerich's costume designs, which were modelled directly on peasant examples housed at Talashkino.

Stravinsky drew widely on relevant folk material in the composition of the music. His principal (but far from exclusive) source was *Melodje ludowe litewskie*, an anthology of Lithuanian folk melodies collected in the nineteenth century by a Polish priest named Anton Juszkiewicz. Stravinsky later gave the impression that the only genuine folk tune in the *Rite* is that played by the high solo bassoon at the opening, a reworking of a Lithuanian melody representing the sound of the *dudki*. The sketches reveal a rather different story. The *Rite* in fact presents a web of folk ideas, weaved into the substance of the music. The melody played by clarinets at the start of the 'Spring Rounds', for example, is a conflation of two more Lithuanian songs, with the addition of some *dudki*-style grace notes. More generally, as Taruskin has revealed, a multitude of melodies can be heard contained within the compass of a perfect fourth, which was characteristic of the *vesnayanki* or springtime songs from the region around Ustilug. Appropriately, they infuse the entire score.[4] In other words, the sources of and models for Stravinsky's music were of a piece with the sources of Roerich's scenario and costume designs. The lies he came to tell about the absence of folk materials in the score were all part of his later concerted effort to reinvent himself as a western European composer.

What is most fascinating about *The Rite of Spring*, however, is the way in which Stravinsky manages to transcend this 'ethnic' material to produce music that, even today, is striking in its modernity. Melodic fragments, whose origins may well be in folk music, are transformed beyond recognition, layered onto each other, resulting in great complexity. Climaxes are built through the accumulation of elements, not by means of progression or development. The famous dissonant 'Rite chord' in the 'Augurs of Spring' is repeated hundreds of times in order to generate a powerful, timeless sense of ritual. ('Will it last a very long time this way?', Diaghilev asked Stravinsky at the first play-through on the piano in Venice. 'To the end, my dear!', replied Stravinsky.) In its novel use of the orchestra, in its bold, mosaic-like formal organization, in its static harmonies and ostinatos, it remains a work of striking originality. Most important of all, though, is the new rhythmic language it invents, suggesting an attitude to time and rhythm that had not been present in Western music since the Middle Ages. The unyielding rhythmic regularity of such sections as the 'Ritual Action of the Ancestors' has a mystical, hypnotic effect. The insistent pulsation of the 'Glorification of the Chosen One' and the 'Sacrificial Dance', organized within constantly shifting metres (a different time-signature in almost every bar), produces music of a disturbing, elemental power. 'There is music whenever there is rhythm, as there is life wherever a pulse beats', Stravinsky

Backdrop by Nicholas Roerich for the American premiere of *The Rite of Spring*, 1930.

Tanztheater Wuppertal perform Pina Bausch's choreography of *The Rite of Spring* at Sadler's Wells, London, 2008.

inscribed in Russian onto a sketch page. The life force of *The Rite of Spring* is its rhythm.

As a musical work the *Rite* began to cast its shadow over composers virtually from the moment it was first heard. Its reputation spread quickly, and – more gradually, once the full score had been published in 1921 – it found its way into the theatres and concert halls of Europe and America. Its influence is evident in music as diverse as that of Edgard Varèse and John Adams, Carl Orff and John Williams, Sergey Prokofiev and Harrison Birtwistle. Even today young composers continue to turn to the score of *The Rite of Spring* as a source of inspiration. In 1940 the music found an entirely new worldwide audience thanks to its inclusion in Disney's animated film *Fantasia*. Cut and reordered, Disney reconceived it as 'a pageant, as the story of the growth of life on Earth'. Though often maligned, Disney's matching of mesmerizing primitive images to the score is a highly effective reimagining of the elemental aspects of the music. While the film imposes a linear narrative absent from the original conception of the work, removing any human or ritualistic character, it nonetheless has a compulsion all of its own. The closing 'Dance of the Earth' sequence remains a persuasive reading. Perhaps Stravinsky even secretly approved of Disney's objectification of the work, 'a coldly accurate reproduction of what science thinks went on during the first few billion years of this planet's existence', as announced by the film's narrator, Deems Taylor. Such a desire for cold accuracy certainly seems to chime with the preference for objective 'execution' over subjective 'interpretation', which Stravinsky had proposed just the previous year in public lectures given at Harvard University in 1939 under the title 'Poetics of Music'. One wonders also if the striking but coincidental resemblance between Disney's colourscapes and Roerich's semi-abstract landscapes resonated with Stravinsky. Roerich's curtain for the 1930 American staged premiere of the *Rite* could easily be mistaken for a still from *Fantasia*.[5]

The Rite of Spring as ballet score inspired some of the most innovative choreographies of the twentieth century. Nijinsky's short-lived interpretation for the premiere performances soon passed into folk memory, not to be revived until the 1980s, when Millicent Hodson and Kenneth Archer reconstructed it for the Joffrey Ballet. With Nijinsky long out of the impresario's favour, Diaghilev commissioned a new choreography from Léonide Massine when the Ballets Russes revived the work for the 1920 season. Subsequently, powerful danced visions have been created by many, including Maurice Béjart, Martha Graham and Angelin Preljocaj. Pre-eminent among them stands Pina Bausch's haunting representation of female victimhood, first made in 1975 by the Tanztheater Wuppertal.

The ending of *The Rite of Spring* is almost unbearable. The machine-like rhythms of the 'Sacrificial Dance' pre-echo the noise and horror of the battlefields of the First World War. For the philosopher Theodor Adorno, a German Jewish émigré writing about Stravinsky in the 1940s, the closing sacrifice of the *Rite* anticipated all too acutely the terrors inflicted on millions of innocents by mid-century totalitarian regimes. Its music overwhelms, it traps, it drives the spectator along with it, so that he or she has no choice but to accept the violence. It is almost as if the viewer becomes a participant in the ritual, complicit in the murder of the Chosen One. By the end, the will of the collective holds sway, annihilating any sense of subjectivity, morality or individual responsibility. This is dangerous music that taps into the deepest, most primitive instincts. It is telling that *The Rite of Spring* remains as powerful for audiences today as it was for those who first heard it in Paris in 1913. A hundred years since its riotous premiere, coloured by the dreadful history of the twentieth century, it continues to shock, excite and bewitch in equal measure.

4

A First Exile: Switzerland,
War and Revolution

In July 1913, less than two months after the premiere in Paris of
The Rite of Spring and recovering from typhoid fever, Stravinsky
travelled to Ustilug once again. He spent the summer there working
on his opera *The Nightingale*, work that he had suspended when he
received the call from Diaghilev to compose *The Firebird*. A year
later he would make another very brief trip to Ustilug and also
to Kiev, principally to collect published Russian folk materials for
Les Noces. It was to be his last visit to the beloved family summer
home. On 28 July 1914 the forces of the Austro-Hungarian Army
began their invasion of Serbia, marking the outbreak of the Great
War. Within a week a new front had opened up with the Russian
Empire on the northeast border of Austria-Hungary. 'The lamps
are going out all over Europe; we shall not see them lit again in
our lifetime', observed the British foreign secretary, Edward Grey,
as two other great European powers, Britain and Germany, also
went to war. It seemed at the time, with good reason, that the
world was about to end. Travel across Europe, especially to the
east, now became virtually impossible. Exempted from military
service on health grounds, Stravinsky would not set foot again
on Russian soil for nearly 50 years. He remained exiled with his
family in neutral Switzerland until the end of the war, and beyond:
first in Clarens (Montreux), then in Leysin in the Vaud Alps, then
in the Pension Bel-Air in Salvan-en-Valois, then back in Clarens in
Villa La Pervenche, rented from the conductor Ernest Ansermet,

with the winter months spent at a hotel in Chateau d'Oex in the Alps. The itinerant life finally came to an end in the spring of 1915, when the Stravinskys rented the Villa Rogivue in Morges on Lake Geneva, where they remained for two years, before moving down the road to La Maison Bornand, a spacious second-floor apartment on Place Saint-Louis, which surely reminded them of their first home on the Kryukov Canal. Diaghilev was only a cycle ride away, having set up a base for the Ballets Russes in Ouchy, south of Lausanne. A motley crew of (mainly) Russian dancers and artists took up residence there. Bakst, Laryonov, Gonchorova, Massine, Nijinsky and others, all Russian émigrés, passed through for sojourns of varying durations. Ansermet was now just a little further round the lake, in Geneva. And it was through Ansermet that Stravinsky would forge a number of new Swiss friendships that were to play an important role in his creative life from now on, principal among them the writer Charles-Ferdinand Ramuz.

One of the first brand new projects Stravinsky contemplated after *The Rite of Spring* was a collaboration with Jean Cocteau. They had initially encountered each other in 1910 in the wings of the theatre in Monte Carlo in which the Ballets Russes had just performed *Le Spectre de la rose*. 'It was in this semi-obscurity, under the moon-light of the lime-lights, that I met Stravinsky', recalls Cocteau. Cocteau had been present at a private rehearsal of *Petrushka* in 1911, and at the premiere of the *Rite*. He was in the company of Stravinsky, Diaghilev, Bakst and Nijinsky after that notorious performance. They had all taken a taxi, late at night, out to the Bois de Boulogne to reflect on the evening's events, and it was this meeting that Cocteau marks as the beginning of their friendship. Together they conceived the idea of a ballet based on rituals from the life of the biblical King David presented as at a contemporary fairground (*The Rite of Spring* meets *Petrushka*, one might say). In spring 1914 Cocteau travelled to Leysin to develop the idea with Stravinsky, who was desperately working to complete

The Nightingale for its premiere by the Ballets Russes at the Paris Opéra that May. It came to nothing. Cocteau confessed that the idea contained both good and bad features, and he congratulated himself 'that circumstances saved us from committing a half-blunder, worse than a blunder'. The idea was not yet ripe. But it generated outcomes, all the same. In some respects it can be understood as a preliminary sketch for Cocteau's circus scenario that was to emerge, spectacularly, in 1917 as *Parade*, staged by the Ballets Russes at the Théâtre du Châtelet, with music by Satie, conducted by Ansermet, designs by Picasso and choreography by Massine, and which impressed Stravinsky. There is evidence to suggest that Stravinsky's *Three Pieces* for string quartet also had their origins in the *David* project, the first of which was composed just a few weeks after Cocteau's visit, and the second of which was prompted by his encounter with the famous clown Little Tich on the London stage in the summer of 1914.

Stravinsky later claimed that these pieces marked an important change in his art. They look forward, he said, to the *Three Easy Pieces* for piano duet (1914–15) and to his neoclassical works. Certainly, as the musicologist Eric Walter White has suggested, there are links between musical ideas in the quartet pieces and three 'symphonies' composed across the next quarter of a century: the *Symphonies of Wind Instruments*, the *Symphony of Psalms* and the Symphony in C.[1] That Stravinsky kept returning to these pieces over a number of years leads one to suspect that they were rather important to him. In 1914 he began orchestrating the first of them, later to become the *Four Studies* for orchestra (with the addition of an orchestration of the *Study* for pianola of 1917). By 1928 these 'abstract' movements had also acquired titles, suggesting further links with the Cocteau project: 'Dance', 'Eccentric' and 'Canticle', plus 'Madrid'. When they were performed in the Aeolian Hall, New York, in 1915 they were grouped together under the title 'Grotesques', pointing towards a parodistic element that was to come to the fore in the music of the Swiss years. Most striking about these pieces is their new simplicity. The first piece might almost be read as a paring right down of *The Rite of Spring*: a concentrated reading of and reflection on, say, the 'Dance of the Earth'. Its main idea on the first violin has the melodic and rhythmic character of a lively, Russian folk dance, joined by a drone in the viola and an accompanying ostinato in the cello, punctuated by a scale fragment in the second violin; the movement's high degree of quasi-mechanical repetition creates a ritual space; and the layering of ideas, each working in its own domain, along with the unchanging harmony, lends the music a static quality. As a whole, the movement is a kind of musical mobile, an object frozen in time: it just starts and stops, but in theory could continue ad infinitum. The music is remarkably prescient. Though already living in Switzerland, Stravinsky wrote these pieces before his final brief trip to Ustilug and before the outbreak of war. Yet he had long sensed that change was imminent. As recorded in the *Autobiography* (albeit by a ghostwriter with the great benefit of hindsight), Stravinsky was 'conscious of the tense atmosphere all over central Europe, and I felt certain that we were on the eve of serious events'. The ironic, distanced, estranged attitude to a representation of dislocated Russian materials in the first of the *Three Pieces* might already be read as the response of an exile, despite the fact that Stravinsky had not yet been irrevocably separated from the motherland.

The change of which Stravinsky spoke is evident in a range of short, instrumental pieces written mainly for piano during his Swiss years: in, for example, the *Valse des fleurs* (1914), *Three Easy Pieces* and *Five Easy Pieces* (1917), all for piano duet, in the *Waltz for Children* (probably 1916) and the pianola *Study*, as well as in *Les Cinq doigts*, again easy pieces for piano and the only work composed in its entirety in 1921 while he and his family were resident at the suburban Paris home of Coco Chanel. That these are primarily pieces for children to play should not deceive us: this is a convenient guise for music that more generally makes a play of simplicity, artifice and expressionlessness, features that would take on far greater significance in the 1920s. Many of these movements feature vamping figures that repeat, mechanically, unchanging, above which diatonic or modal melodies meander in a directionless manner, often clashing humorously with the accompaniment. (It is hardly surprising that Stravinsky took such close interest in the mechanical pianola during these years.) His models are genre pieces: waltzes, polkas, marches. The melodies are taken from all over: Russia, Ireland, Italy, Spain. The influence of Satie is clear. The two first met in 1911 and they continued to move in the same circles. Stravinsky liked him, and the second of the *Three Easy Pieces* is dedicated to him (a waltz, like so many Satie had written). Though Stravinsky rarely made public reference to Satie, these Swiss piano pieces echo the simplicity and stasis of Satie's 'vamping' *Gymnopédies* and *Gnossiennes* from as early as the 1880s, his predilection for parodying genre pieces, and even his 'childish' music written as recently as 1913 (*Enfantillages pittoresques*, *Menus propos enfantines* and *Trois nouvelles enfantines*). Satie's poses are not so far removed from Stravinsky's. After all, Stravinsky had already demonstrated in *Petrushka* that he could 'do' parody and the grotesque by means of a musical stasis. But what is so fascinating about these pieces is how they reveal Stravinsky's modernist attitude to his material, whatever its provenance, as will become increasingly apparent in works from *Pulcinella* (1919–20) onwards.

Satie often used popular musical models in his music, as well as leading a double life as a composer of cabaret songs and *café-concert* music. Stravinsky had long been an habitué of nightclubs, music halls and cafés (a practice he had picked up from Diaghilev in St Petersburg), and there he would have become familiar with the most recent American popular music of ragtime and early jazz, which was taking Paris by storm. He also acquired some recordings (in part thanks to Ansermet, who brought back sheet music and records for Stravinsky from his 1916 tour of America with the Ballets Russes). At one level one might say that this 'jazz' was just one more exotic *objet trouvé* that he could treat in his own manner, as he had done in *Petrushka*, and more recently in the 'Española' and 'Napolitana' of the *Five Easy Pieces*. But it was more than this. In the generic language of ragtime – a virtuosic piano style with a rich rhythmic language, making prominent use of syncopation and dotted notes – Stravinsky found echoes of his own practices. And ragtime and jazz were modern, chic, Western. In aligning himself with such music, Stravinsky was as good as clothing himself in the latest Paris fashions. Just as in the simplification of the children's piano pieces, the references to jazz styles are perhaps an early sign of Stravinsky confronting his status as émigré, of his desire to be assimilated to his host francophone culture. Three little rags emerged during the war years and just after. The most telling of these concludes a set of three popular dances, 'Tango – Waltz – Ragtime', that forms part of *The Soldier's Tale*, 'a parable both of the times in which it was written and Stravinsky's predicament as a prisoner of those times'.[2] To the accompaniment of untuned percussion and double bass, the virtuosic violin swings into life in characteristic ragtime style; yet, all too soon, Stravinsky appears to glance backwards as the music gets caught up in unyielding repetitions within a continually changing metre that shouts of a folk fiddler playing a very different kind of Russian dance.

Russia was inevitably on Stravinsky's mind during the war years. In the final year of the war his thoughts turned to a story about a soldier, which he set about telling with the help of Ramuz. Stravinsky relates how the project was born of straitened wartime circumstances, when the two artists came up with the idea of a small-scale travelling theatre piece for narrator, dancer and a small ensemble of musicians and actors. Its source was the story of a runaway soldier and the Devil found in an Afanas'yev collection of Russian folk tales, though it also reverberated more widely through European (Faustian) legend. It told of the soldier who sells his violin to the Devil in exchange for a book that can predict the future. It brings him wealth but not happiness. The soldier beats the Devil at a game of cards and wins back his violin, which he plays to cure a princess of her illness so that he may marry her. But nostalgia gets the better of him and the soldier is finally recaptured by the Devil as he attempts to return to his native land. Thus the tale had all the ingredients to make it pertinent to its time: '*Our* soldier, in 1918, was very definitely understood to be the victim of the then world conflict', recalled the composer much later. For Stravinsky, a story of the longing of the exile for the homeland in which a violin is given the central role was especially poignant. Taruskin goes further and argues that *The Soldier's Tale* 'may be read as a parable of the Russian Revolution as viewed from afar and with dismay by Stravinsky who had greeted the events of February 1917 as a liberation, only to see that brief interlude of freedom dashed by a coup'.[3]

The Soldier's Tale is one of the most innovative and influential of twentieth-century works of music-theatre. It stands as the exemplar of a new genre – straddling as it does concert work and theatre – which went on to flourish across the century. Stravinsky knew all about street theatre and itinerant musicians, as *Petrushka* had revealed, but here they are deployed to create a rough theatre, very different from the luxurious productions of the Ballets Russes. There are just seven players whose make-up (violin and bass, clarinet and bassoon, cornet and trombone, plus percussion) alludes to a variety of popular and peasant combos, and who play an eclectic mix of music that ranges across Europe and Russia, high art and popular, sacred and secular. It is veritable theatre music but theatre music in which the musicians, rather than being hidden, play an active role. 'The violin is the soldier's soul, and

Robert Delaunay, *Igor Stravinsky*, 1918.

the drums are the *diablerie*.' The narrator is crucial, acting as
a chorus figure, 'a two-way go-between: that is . . . someone who
is an illusionist interpreter between the characters themselves,
as well as a commentator between the stage and the audience',
as Stravinsky later observed. His most important function is one
of distancing the audience from the tale. This is not naturalistic
theatre. The narrative is disrupted, just as the music is a kind of

collage of musical allusion; the audience is alienated. In these respects *The Soldier's Tale* is a landmark for Stravinsky in that (with *Petrushka* as an important precursor) it anticipates the eclecticism of the neoclassical works and, in making such a play of distance, draws the theme of exile into the very musical substance of the work.

The war years in Switzerland were undeniably difficult for Stravinsky. He describes the end of 1917 as one of the hardest periods he had ever experienced:

> Overwhelmed by the successive bereavements I had suffered, I was now also in a position of the utmost pecuniary difficulty. The Communist Revolution, which had just triumphed in Russia, deprived me of the last resources which had still from time to time been reaching me from the country, and I found myself, so to speak, face to face with nothing, in a foreign land and right in the middle of the war.[4]

Catherine had been diagnosed with tuberculosis and was sent to a sanatorium, which is how the family had found itself caught in Switzerland at the outbreak of war. The suspension of the activities of the Ballets Russes in Paris denied Stravinsky a significant source of income. Royalties from other performances were also severely curtailed, though he did discover the beginnings of a new source of income through conducting, making his debut on the podium in Geneva in 1915 with the *Firebird* suite. In the early years of the war his mother, Anna Kyrillovna, who had been with them in Switzerland, was anxious to return to St Petersburg (now renamed Petrograd), where she remained cut off from Stravinsky during the entire war. As the war dragged on and with the coming to power of the Bolsheviks after the October revolutions, Stravinsky lost virtually everything. The family estate at Ustilug had been looted and destroyed in 1915 by the combined Austro-Hungarian and German armies, which saw the end to any income flowing from investments the Stravinskys had made there, including in a Ukrainian vodka business. The Belyankins, who were still living there, were forced out and by a tortuous route over three years eventually made their way to Switzerland to take up residence with the Stravinskys at Maison Bornand. The death in 1917 of his childhood *nyanya*, Bertha, who was living with them in Morges and taking care of Stravinsky's children, hit him hard. His grief was compounded when, just three months later, he learned of the death of his brother Gury from typhus while serving in Romania with a Red Cross unit.

These years, then, were a time of deep emotion and profound loss for Stravinsky. Above all else, he realized that he would not be making an early return to his motherland. His response was to immerse himself more deeply than ever before in his native culture. Like so many exiles before him, he set about recreating in his imagination the home he had lost.

Stravinsky 'found some alleviation' in the delight with which he steeped himself in Russian folk poems. Across the Swiss years he produced a large number of songs, settings of Russian texts discovered in the published anthologies of Afanas'yev, Pyotr Kireyevsky, Ivan Sakharov and others, and grouped into song collections: these include a set of four *Pribaoutki* (1914), four *Cat's Cradle Songs* (1915), *Four Russian Peasant Songs* (1914–17), *Trois histoires pour enfants* (1915/17) in Ramuz's translation, and *Four Russian Songs* (1918–19). Many of the texts he chose carried particular resonance in their expression of longing and alienation: 'The sparrow looks in someone else's direction [to the foreign side]'; 'Closed are my ways to Thy Kingdom'. Absorbed in the study of Russian folk music, Stravinsky made a breakthrough realization, as he later recalled:

One important characteristic of Russian popular verse is that the accents of the spoken verse are ignored when the verse is sung. The recognition of the musical possibilities inherent in this fact was one of the most rejoicing discoveries of my life.

Although shifting accents had already emerged as highly significant in his music (the 'Augurs of Spring' from the *Rite* being just the most obvious example), Stravinsky now 'discovered' that he could handle texts in the same way, derived from an understanding of Russian folk verse where accents could be treated flexibly in relation to 'natural' speech accents and musical metre. Texts could be regarded merely as language, as sources of sonic rather than semantic material, where stress could be exploited like any other aspect of the music. Many of the song texts he set are nonsense rhymes and riddles ('Tilim-bom'), with which he developed a playful relationship. These became his compositional workshop. He adopted the same attitude to other texts where semantics and narrative would appear more significant, yet with the result that the listener is distanced from the meaning. It is an extraordinary strategy of alienation that would remain with Stravinsky for the rest of his composing career, in whichever language he chose to work.

Stravinsky's response to exile, then, would appear Janus-faced, looking to the future in his simple piano pieces by seeming to abandon Russia, looking to the past in his songs by immersing himself deeply in folk traditions. Such dualism remained a striking aspect of his creative output even in the 1920s. Yet the reception of Stravinsky's relationship with his native culture has been complicated by his later attempts at denying its importance: in the 1950s, for instance, he observed to Craft that 'I could never share his [Bartók's] lifelong gusto for his native folklore. This devotion was certainly real and touching, but I couldn't help regretting it in the great musician.' 'Never' is clearly an untruth. On his return to Russia only a few years later he confessed to the deep influence of Russian language and culture across his entire life. Ever the opportunist, Stravinsky told his audiences what he thought they wanted to hear. But the contradictions are intriguing. In fact, what one detects in the music of the Swiss years is a powerful expression of loss through the refinement of techniques he had already developed in *Petrushka* and *The Rite of Spring*: distancing and alienation, parody and irony, stasis achieved through the obsessive working of small musical motifs and pedal points. Sometimes this manifested itself directly as lament; at other times it emerged as a humour tinged with sadness. Both modes are apparent in the piano pieces and the songs.

All this play with verse and language led to two major Russian works. *Renard*, composed in 1915–16, is an amalgam of children's songs and nonsense rhymes found in Afanas'yev, where text and music were forged side by side. This 'Tale About the Fox, the Cock, the Tomcat and the Ram' (later a 'Goat' in the French translation by Ramuz) is, like *Petrushka*, subtitled 'A Burlesque', and emerges as a kind of rough pantomime, to be performed by clowns, dancers or acrobats on a trestle table with the orchestra and singers behind it. The singers are not specifically identified with any of the four mimed or danced characters, and in their stylized song and speech remain distanced, occasionally even commenting on the action. This distancing is reinforced by the framing device of the march, by means of which the players are led into and out of the performing space. It is made quite clear that this is theatre and not real life. The peasant band contains a cimbalom, the stringed instrument of Hungarian provenance that Stravinsky first heard and fell in love with in 1915 while dining one evening with Ansermet at a Geneva restaurant. It comically represents the goat, as well as imitating the sound of the *gusli*, a kind of balalaika. Or so Stravinsky claimed. In fact it would seem that the cimbalom music is an invention rather than being based on any actual Russian folk tradition. *Renard* reveals itself as the product of the nostalgic imagination, Stravinsky's exile from country, culture and family manifesting itself in a work that is simultaneously of and not of

Russia. As in the little Swiss piano pieces, the humour here, the nonsense, as well as the exuberant textual playfulness, is a defensive strategy that attempts to mask Stravinsky's 'sense of sadness at being so distant from my country', as he later recorded in the *Autobiography*.

The work, however, that dominated Stravinsky's early years of exile was perhaps the most profoundly Russian of any he ever composed: *Svadebka*, to use its Russian title, or *Les Noces* (The Wedding) as it is more generally known from the translation into French by Ramuz. The first thoughts for the work pre-date his exile, from 1912, while he was still working on Part Two of *The Rite of Spring*; its composition was continually interrupted, and though a preliminary sketch was finished in 1917, it was not finally completed and premiered until 1923, when it was given on 13 June in Paris by the Ballets Russes, with designs by Natalia Goncharova and choreography by Nijinsky's sister Bronislava Nijinska. Its long gestation was an understandable consequence of the difficult circumstances of the war years and the problems in securing performances of works for large forces. But this only accounts in part for the radical shift in the character of *Les Noces* from, initially, a lavish, narrative representation of a Russian peasant wedding to, eventually, a stylized, non-narrative ritual action. The story of the work's evolution shadows the composer's own changing relationship with Russia in exile (corresponding, indeed, with the rapid change in identity of Russia itself) away from a 'real' and towards an imagined motherland.

The most obvious change was in the scoring. It began in the manner of the imposing works of the Ballets Russes repertoire with a vast *Rite*-size orchestra, pitting great blocks of instruments against each other, later planned as separate groups of instruments arranged about the stage. This proved impracticable so Stravinsky tried a pared-down *Renard*-style chamber ensemble. That, too, was eventually rejected in favour of a 'simpler' version, which introduced two cimbaloms alongside other percussion, and where wind and string instruments were replaced by a harmonium and pianola respectively. Stravinsky adopted this solution not least, one imagines, because the use of mechanical instruments corresponded with the shift in character of the work as a whole towards something more objectified and ritualistic – 'impersonal', to use Stravinsky's word. Indeed, the presence of electrically operated instruments here brings to the fore those mechanical aspects that had been such a feature of *The Rite of Spring*. Despite its apparently comic and celebratory tone, *Les Noces* has much in common with its darker predecessor, all the way through to the final 'sacrifice' of the virgin overseen by the elders. ('After Fetis and Nastasia have been escorted to the bedroom, they are left alone, and the door is closed. The two fathers and two mothers seat themselves on a bench in front of the door, and all the wedding guests face them.') Loss and lament are central to *Les Noces*, 'disquiet in the face of the twofold mystery of life ending and life beginning', as Roman Vlad observes; *Les Noces* resembles the *Rite* in 'the expression of pain which overtakes mankind at the contemplation of the dread forces by which it is surrounded'.[5] It is thus revealed very much as a product of the war years, thrown into relief by the radiance and extraordinary stasis of the closing bell chimes, at the same time a nostalgic memory of Petersburg (albeit prompted by hearing the bells of St Paul's Cathedral from a London taxi) and a representation of a kind of forgetting.

In the end, Stravinsky also had to reject his preferred scoring for practical reasons: it proved impossible in performance to synchronize the pianola with the non-mechanical instruments. Nonetheless, the final version for four pianos and large percussion ensemble retains a percussive brilliance, whose hard-edged, jewelled sounds perfectly support the ceremonial chanting of choir and soloists. The text was crafted by Stravinsky into a sequence of four tableaux from the ethnographic materials he had collected on his last trip to Ustilug and Kiev, principally Kireyevsky's great collection of popular Russian lyrics, and with which he had already been experimenting in his songs. Laments and prayers are woven into episodes from the wedding (the preparation of bride and groom, the bride's departure, the wedding feast and the consummation of the marriage). The action is always symbolic: as in *Renard*, no soloist is identified consistently with any character. While rooted in authentic examples, the melodic material is, for the most part, freely invented. The lament for the maiden's tresses at the very start, for example, with its characteristic 'sobbing' grace notes, evokes actual music sung by peasant brides. The striking non-tonal harmony of *Les Noces* – which might crudely be described as 'modal', a blend of anhemitonic, diatonic and octatonic scale forms – is also derived from his study of folk materials. Above all, what gives the work its energy is its rhythmic organization, stemming first and foremost from Stravinsky's response to the stresses of the text. Rhythm is every much the primary structural agent here, as it had been for *The Rite of Spring*. It is music with the most powerful momentum that drives forwards, relentlessly, at once ritual orgy and tragic dance. It is ultimately Stravinsky's most glorious celebration of Russia, but a Russia imagined and invented at a great distance, in exile.

5

A Creative Epiphany: Paris Style and Neoclassicism

Igor Stravinsky. Portrait by Jacques-Émile Blanche. 1915. On the shore of the fashionable resort of Deauville, pausing just for a moment before moving on to his next society engagement, stands Stravinsky the French dandy. He is sporting a bow-tie, blazer and handkerchief, neatly creased trousers with turn-ups and spats. His shirt is undoubtedly made of silk. Over his arm a brown coat hangs loosely as he clutches a felt Homburg. His look is preoccupied, as befits a serious artist, his expression exaggerated by a pencil moustache lining his upper lip. The wooden cane on which he leans is an accessory long in vogue with the gentry. A sophisticated modern man looks back at us, tall, elegant, aristocratic, in command of himself and his image.

The imprimatur of Blanche, a respected society portrait painter, was important for Stravinsky. He did the great service of representing the composer as he wished himself to be seen. The spectator's viewpoint is here placed relatively low to exaggerate the subject's height. The reality was rather different. Just 160 centimetres tall (5 feet 3 inches), Stravinsky had been deeply sensitive about his diminutive stature all his adult life. Maybe his preoccupation with a stylish, expensive and aggrandizing appearance in imitation of an upper-class gentleman was a defensive strategy of distraction.

From around the same time as Blanche's portrait comes a rather different picture of Stravinsky recorded by Romain Rolland:

Jacques-Émile Blanche, *Igor Stravinsky*, 1915.

He is small, sickly looking, ugly, yellow-faced, thin and tired, with a narrow brow, thin, receding hair, his eyes screwed up behind a pince-nez, a fleshy nose, big lips, a disproportionately long face in relation to his forehead.[1]

Beneath his clothes, however, his body was lean and lithe. This is confirmed by a photograph from 1930 of the composer approaching the age of 50, alongside his son Theodore, both displaying their youthful, bronzed, muscular torsos. Stravinsky had always been vain to the point of narcissism. His daily regimen throughout most of his life began with physical exercise. He clearly took care of his body. And he obviously enjoyed posing for photographs. He was not even immodest about sharing with family members photographs of himself in the nude – immodest, verging on cruel, it might be said, given that some of these pictures were taken by his mistress Vera Sudeykina while he was on holiday with her and not his wife.

Stravinsky's family, friends and professional acquaintances were often struck by his appearance and recorded this in letters and diaries. Newspapers frequently commented on his sartorial choices. His niece Tanya, who lived with the family for almost a year in the mid-1920s, was a keen chronicler of her uncle's wardrobe: 'He dresses stunningly and has a vast number of neckties', she wrote to her parents.[2] In 1924 Jean Cocteau catalogued Stravinsky's many modish accessories, but was also quick to recognize that these were just a part of his world of appearances:

Rings, gaiters, scarves, half-belts, ties, tiepins, wristwatches, mufflers, fetishes, pinces-nez [sic], monocles, glasses, chain bracelets, describe him badly. Put simply, they prove on the surface that Stravinsky goes out of his way for no one. He composes, dresses himself, and speaks as he wishes.[3]

They may well prove that. But these various portraits also demonstrate just how far it mattered to Stravinsky to be attired *à la mode du moment*. Part of this may well have been motivated by a fear of being perceived as provincial, as out of step with sophisticated post-war Paris society, a feeling that lay equally behind his musical move in the 1920s away from Russia and towards an alignment with the classics of western European music. But principally it was because he was a man of his time, in dress sense as well as in music, and he wanted above all else to be recognized as a modern.

Stravinsky's cult of self and body reinforced an obsession with his own health that stemmed from his childhood. Like his mother, he was a hypochondriac. On a number of occasions in his life, though, he came close to death, most famously following the premiere performances of *The Rite of Spring* when, apparently after eating a bad oyster, he contracted typhoid fever, the same infection that killed his brother Gury just four years later. Medical bills and who was to pay them are a recurring motif of his correspondence. But he did not help himself with his fondness for cigarettes, fine wine and convivial dining. This was all part and parcel of being with the in-crowd. In St Petersburg he had already developed a penchant for the nightclub, and it was at such venues in Paris that he would meet the influential people who liked to keep the company of this celebrity composer and who, in turn, would be most useful to him. The drunken celebration that followed the successful opening of *Pulcinella* at the Opéra in 1920 is just one example of the many wild, society evenings in which he participated. It is also possible (though accounts vary) that it was on this particular occasion that Diaghilev introduced Stravinsky to Gabrielle 'Coco' Chanel.

Cigarettes were an important part of the image Stravinsky projected. He used a long, gently curved cigarette holder made, as Theodore recalls his father telling the family, 'from the beak of an albatross', 'very, very valuable', and with which he was frequently photographed. The cigarette had become as much a symbol of desirable, liberal, post-war chic as the flapper and the motor car, especially since it was increasingly marketed at and smoked by women. Again it mattered to Stravinsky that he was seen to be part of that modern society. His dress and his manner were part of this assimilation. Paris had fallen in love with Stravinsky on the night of the premiere of *The Firebird* in 1910, and Stravinsky fell in love with Paris. From then on, until he set sail in 1939 to live permanently in the United States, Stravinsky's success was intimately tied up with the life of the City of Light.

Fashion is more than just the vogue for a certain manner of dress and behaviour in a particular place or time; it is the cultural construction of identity. It is in this context that an examination of the reciprocal relationship between the changes in both Stravinsky's dress and music and the wider cultural and social changes in the world he inhabited can be instructive. The writing of Mary E. Davis has been particularly influential in helping to reconfigure an understanding of post-war art in the wider Paris environment. Her work centres on Paris fashion and couturiers, and the magazines that promoted and celebrated them. In brief, she argues for the profound significance of the linked endeavours of music and fashion to modernist thought. The salons and cabarets, the theatres, concert halls and galleries of Paris provided the setting in which moved some of the most influential thinkers and artists of the interwar years, along with the wealthiest patrons of the arts in the upper echelons of French society. The fashion press carried discussion of the latest trends in music, just as the music of Stravinsky and others 'shared [an] engagement with [the] broader culture of style that prevailed in elite Parisian circles after the war'. At the heart of Davis's argument is the notion of *chic*, initially signifying modern elegance in general and, after 1914,

Gabrielle 'Coco' Chanel, *c*. 1925.

taking on more specific associations of the 'youthful', of 'ingenuous grace', 'harmonious and discrete [*sic*] simplicity', and charm.[4]

　　Pre-eminent among the leaders of the post-war fashion revolution was Chanel. She enters this story directly in the context of the affair that she apparently conducted with Stravinsky in 1920, a liaison which, though the subject of much speculation and inevitable exaggeration, including a successful novel and film, is not supported by any independent evidence beyond the anecdotal.[5] It was not until 1946 that Chanel made a confession to Paul Morand, and he did not publish it until 30 years after that, when Coco and Igor were both dead. In any case, it would seem that Chanel was as adept at reinventing her own past as was Stravinsky. Nonetheless, given the propensities of both parties, there is little reason to doubt the powerful attraction between the two: 'Igor is flighty, Chanel seductive', reflected Denise Stravinsky, on the authority of her husband, Theodore. In the autumn of 1920 Chanel invited the impoverished Stravinsky family and entourage to move from Brittany (where they had recently relocated after their long wartime sojourn in Switzerland) to take up residence in Bel Respiro, her newly acquired Art Nouveau villa in the western Paris suburb of Garches. (Chanel herself was living in a grand suite at the Ritz Hotel on Place Vendôme.) She was an admirer of his work, having first encountered his music at the preview of *The Rite of Spring* in 1913, and now made a significant donation to enable Diaghilev to mount the new production choreographed by Massine. The affair allegedly began soon after the composer's installation in Bel Respiro. Such a situation was unsustainable long term, and so by the following spring, on the pretext of Catherine's fragile health, the family moved to Biarritz – fashionable, certainly, and the location of Chanel's second shop, opened in 1915, but about as far as it was possible to be from Paris while remaining within the French borders. Stravinsky maintained a base in the capital city thanks to a studio provided by the Pleyel piano company, situated above their workshops on rue Rochechouart. Music, business and affairs could now be conducted safely away from the gaze of his family. But he was in conflict with himself. However much time he spent in Paris, he would always refer to '*chez moi*' as where Catherine and the family were.

There were other women besides Chanel and before Stravinsky had met and fallen head-over-heels in love with Vera Sudeykina, his future mistress and second wife – among them, two young Russian dancers, first Lydia Lopukhova, then Zhenya Nikitina at the Chauve-Souris cabaret; a Brazilian singer, Vera Janacopoulos; and the famously beautiful Juanita Gandarillas. At one level, knowledge of Stravinsky's personal misdemeanours has scant critical bearing on an understanding of his creative work, aside from indicating a weakness in sexual matters that contrasted sharply with the near-compulsive orderliness of his daily routines – one of the many contradictions that defined the man. Yet, at another level, it suggests that he was as adept at wearing masks in his private life as he was in public. Liaisons with glamorous women fed his desire to be adored. It is perfectly possible that he was totally calculating about his relationships – 'logical, as opposed to psychological' is how Craft describes him.[6] Though he relied utterly on Catherine, she was just another reminder of his provincial Russian origins, which he wanted to conceal as best he could. She did not fit his public persona. For eighteen years until Catherine's death in 1939, it was the beautiful blue-eyed Vera who shared the limelight with the composer as his public escort, touring Europe and America with him, attending premieres, being seen at all the fashionable events and glamorous locations, photographed by the press. A physically weak Catherine, continually struggling with the pulmonary diseases that would eventually claim her life, was kept at a distance, managing the home, caring for their children and his mother. Ironically, for the sake of good form, it was Vera whom Stravinsky called his 'secretary', when it was more properly Catherine who fulfilled that role as his trusted copyist and musical adviser. He thus led an extraordinary double life. One can see the advantages to Stravinsky: the celebrity lifestyle in Paris with Vera; the supportive family life at home with Catherine – where, in fact, he did most of his composing.

Catherine endured the situation with fortitude and public dignity, no doubt for the sake of her children, and because she had little alternative. Milène, Stravinsky's beloved youngest child, recalls a trip to Paris in 1933 with her mother to be introduced to her father's 'lady'. She was told by Catherine that she must not think ill of either of them. 'Never have I seen her cry like that', recollects Milène after their return home. Perhaps Catherine felt that such suffering was an inescapable part of the Russian character, and that she had a religious duty stoically to support her husband's creative talent, come what may. 'Temptations and trials are good for the soul', she wrote in 1935 in a letter to Stravinsky from her sanatorium in Sancellemoz. Yet Stravinsky's emotional abuse clearly took its toll. Denise writes of a 'veil of sadness drawn forever over her beautiful face', of her 'torment' and the 'wound that would never heal'. But the family also seemed eager to emphasize that 'Igor would also suffer this torment for which he knew he was himself responsible', and he would tenderly console his wife. It was a peculiar kind of self-imposed suffering, no doubt driven by guilt, compounded by the emotional pressure to keep the affair entirely hidden from his mother. Did Stravinsky really love and need both women equally, simultaneously, though in different ways? It is certainly true that he was genuinely paralysed with grief at Catherine's death. All one can say is that, whatever they thought of the situation and whatever their feelings towards Vera, the children did not wish their father to be shown in a bad light. As Theodore and Denise's testimony confirms, they wanted him to be remembered first and foremost as a loving family man.

And what of Stravinsky's relationships with men? Inevitably for the age in which he lived, his student and early professional life was homosocial. The communities of artists and intellectuals in which he moved, and which were vital to support and promote his work, were almost exclusively male, from the *Mir iskusstva* group in Petersburg to his involvement with the Les Apaches group in Paris. Close relationships developed between these men, and ruptures in friendships – such as, most famously, Stravinsky's with Diaghilev – were felt intensely. Many of these men were gay, and some, like Diaghilev, were entirely open about their gay relationships. Stravinsky was clearly very fond of them, as indeed he was of his favourite brother Gury, who was also gay. But, to date, nothing suggests that Stravinsky was sexually involved with any of these men. Robert Craft made the surprising claim in 2013 that 'in the early Diaghilev period Stravinsky was exclusively in an ambisexual phase'.[7] Aside from the awkwardness of the locution (how can one be exclusively attracted to persons of either sex?), he offers no evidence, save from some dubious translations and misleading interpretations of letters that have long been in the public domain. Craft proposes that affairs took place with Andrey Rimsky-Korsakov and the composer Maurice Delage (who, *pace* Craft, was French, not Belgian). Most surprising of all is his claim that 'Ravel and Stravinsky were time-to-time lovers', without a jot of documentation to support it.[8] The most surprising aspect of Craft's so-called revelations is that there had not been the slightest whisper of this as an issue until the second decade of the twenty-first century. If Stravinsky had been conducting passionate affairs with men, even for a short period, then his friends are hardly likely to have kept the gossip to themselves. Until such time as Craft produces convincing new evidence, one has to remain suspicious of the motives of this otherwise indispensable figure in making sense of Stravinsky's life and legacy.

Biarritz and Nice, following the family's move there in 1924, were important to Stravinsky for another reason. Like Paris, they both had significant émigré Russian communities, especially after the mass exodus of White Russians in the wake of the Revolution. However much the darling of cosmopolitan Paris society may have been embarrassed by his provincial past, domestically Stravinsky maintained the strongest of ties with the culture of the motherland. Neither Igor nor Catherine had been observant members of the Orthodox church for some time, but according to Denise they

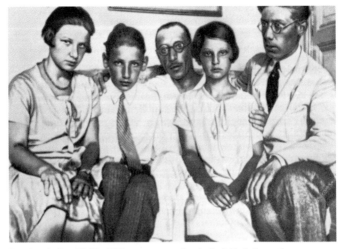

Igor Stravinsky with his children, 1926. L–R: Lyudmila (Mika), Svyatoslav (Soulima), I.S., Milena (Milène), Fyodor (Theodore).

retained their faith. There was a large Orthodox church in Biarritz, where Milène made her first confession and where, increasingly, the long-suffering Catherine sought spiritual solace. In Nice, too, there was an important Orthodox colony. Here, for a while, the entire family attended the branch of the Russian church that, after 1917, became known as the 'Église hors frontières' or 'Church in Exile'. The family home as a piece of old Russia (Ustilug, even) translated first to Swiss, then to French soil: not just Igor, Catherine and the four children, their faithful *nyanya*, Bertha Essen (replaced after her death in Morges by 'Madubo'), and their staff, but also the Belyankins, with their own *nyanya*, who had first taken refuge with the Stravinskys in Morges. The 'in-laws' then moved with them to Brittany, to Bel Respiro and to Biarritz, before their ways parted. In 1922 Stravinsky's mother left what was now Petrograd to return to the bosom of the family in exile. It was she more than anyone in this itinerant tribe who kept the spirit of Russia alive. Anna and Catherine did their best to make wherever they lived уютный, 'uyutnyi' ('an excellent Russian word', as Denise Stravinsky describes it, representing the atmosphere of the Stravinsky home, a word that 'signifies charm, intimacy . . . and something more too, as in the German *gemütlich*'[9]). Catherine would spend her evenings embroidering traditional icons in gold and silver thread. Anna would always serve visitors tea and proper Russian snacks. She outlived – albeit very briefly – both her daughter-in-law Catherine and her granddaughter Mika, and was finally laid to rest in June 1939 next to them both in the Russian Orthodox cemetery at Sainte-Geneviève-des-Bois outside Paris.

Thus, despite appearances to the contrary in these post-war years, when Paris chic was an important focus of his public energies, Russia remained a fundamental and continuous part of Stravinsky's private existence. This reinforces Richard Taruskin's influential thesis, namely that, whatever the varied musical surfaces might suggest, the composer's 'deeply ingrained habits of Russian thinking and hearing' held sway throughout his creative life. Late in life, Stravinsky himself came to acknowledge that his fundamental *slog* (style or manner) had always been *russkiy*, through and through.[10] But there was clearly a tension between the two worlds, between Stravinsky's desire to be modern, and his sense of his patrimony. Such tension between past and present is a mark of estrangement, of exile. It played itself out in complex ways across Stravinsky's life and work.

To return to interwar Paris. Stravinsky's presence in the ambit of Chanel – affair or otherwise – is highly significant given that, in Davis's words, she played such a 'vital role in forging and advancing an ideal of artistic modernism based in simplicity and everyday elegance'.[11] The *style dépouillé* ('stripped away', meaning plain, without ornament) of the 1920s found its most influential expression in Chanel's little black dress, which swiftly became an emblem of the age: simple lines, demure, elegant, a 'classic' from the moment it emerged, yet in principle accessible to all. On 1 October 1926 *Vogue* famously proclaimed it as 'The Chanel "Ford" – the frock that all the world will wear'. Like the Ford Model T motor car, it symbolized a liberated personal style in the modern world of mass-production and consumption. In this context, it is clear that the changes that took place in Stravinsky's music during and after the First World War – a paring away of the inessential, a move towards a greater simplicity and purity – were inextricably tied up with the characteristics of chic that prevailed in contemporary haute couture. Similarly, the eclecticism that defines interwar Art Deco fashion defines the modernism of Stravinsky's so-called neoclassicism too. Stravinsky's neoclassical chic spoke in much the same way to the Paris socialites and celebrities, the Bright Young People of *les années folles*, as did the popular dance music of the Jazz Age and the designs of Chanel.

The *Vogue* fashion plate illustrating Chanel's black dress is framed by the simple, geometric lines characteristic of the Art Deco graphic style. That the achievements of high fashion of the 1920s were part of the broader style that later became known as Art Deco is made abundantly clear by the illustrated cover of the visitors' guide to the 1925 Paris Exhibition, the Exposition Internationale des Arts Décoratifs et Industriels Modernes.[12] Paris and its buildings are relegated to the background, while in the foreground stands a young woman attired in the latest streamlined coat, hat, shoes and jewellery. It is striking that she is to be found not in the context of industrial concrete, steel and glass but beside a simple white column topped with a version of an Ionic capital: the modern in dialogue with the past. Fashion played a central role in the 1925 Exhibition. Couture was presented not just as commerce but as one of the *arts décoratifs modernes*. According to the guide, fashion 'set the pace for other media' and was 'critical to "*la modernité*" existing as it did on "*surprise et nouveauté*"'.[13] Art Deco in general came to stand for modernity in Paris. This post-war

Théâtre des Champs-Élysées, avenue Montaigne, Paris.

period of rapid social, political and economic change was driven
by technological innovation, and Art Deco responded to this:
indeed, it provided the new buildings demanded by the new
age, such as public meeting and exhibition spaces (the Palais
de Chaillot), cinemas (the Secrétan Palace) and an airport (Le
Bourget). Paris architects of the 1920s and '30s envisaged a vibrant
urban environment, resolutely modern, monumental, accessible.
The new technology of the motor car, the aeroplane and the ocean
liner opened up the world, and the Art Deco style refracted this in
its internationalism and its eclecticism. And that same technology
enabled the rapid dissemination of Paris modernism around the
world – to London, to New York, to Mumbai, Shanghai and
Melbourne – such that Art Deco became the first truly international
art style. Art Deco in its many guises captured the 'high' West
and the 'exotic' East, the elite and the mass-produced, the abstract

and the decorative. There are again salient resonances with the interwar neoclassical Stravinsky, positioned between high and low, between progressive and conservative.

It was in this Paris milieu that Stravinsky moved and worked. His music was made for some of the most significant new buildings in Paris, and inevitably his thinking was in part formed by and interpreted that modern environment. Take, by way of illustration, one of the most important public buildings erected in Paris in the years leading up to the First World War and whose history is indelibly interleaved with that of Stravinsky. The Théâtre des Champs-Élysées on the fashionable avenue Montaigne, site of the premiere of *The Rite of Spring* on 29 May 1913, had made its own debut just a few weeks earlier. Designed by the architect brothers Auguste and Gustave Perret, it displays many of the characteristics that later came to be associated with Art Deco. It is a bold statement that looks both to the future by rejecting Romanticism and the opulent belle époque style, and back to the classical past. The brothers used the word *dépouillé* to describe the character of the building. The exterior is simple, austere, unemotional,

La Danse, bas-relief sculpture by Antoine Bourdelle, above the entrance to the Comédie auditorium, Théâtre des Champs-Élysées.

monumental and elegant. Its modernism springs not just from its primary building material (reinforced concrete) but from the severity of its clear, geometrical lines and lack of overt exterior decoration, save the gilt-edged windows and the frieze. Yet it also looks back to antiquity, not through pastiche of the ancient Greek temple, but by reinterpreting the idea and function of columns and tympanum. The bas-relief carvings of the triptych entitled *Apollon et sa méditation* are by the artist Antoine Bourdelle and give another modernist reading of antique subject-matter. Again in these sculptures is to be found an interest in strong geometries, intense simplification and a tendency towards abstraction. The pared-down style and the references to the classical past invoke a sense of purity that looks forward strongly to the aesthetic concerns of the post-war age, in such works as Satie's *Socrate*, a setting of excerpts from Plato's *Dialogues* written towards the end of the war. Satie called it a 'return to classical simplicity with a modern sensibility'. When Stravinsky first heard it in 1919, he was apparently deeply impressed.

To the right of the theatre's main entrance, above the doors leading to the smaller *Comédie* auditorium, is a further set of bas-relief sculptures by Bourdelle. One is called *La Danse* and depicts in the guise of a classical god and goddess Vaslav Nijinsky and Isadora Duncan, the two most progressive dancers of the day. It is a celebration of youth, of the modern. *La Danse* is defined by simplicity of line and a classical purity, but with a highly charged eroticism and an implicit violence. Like the *Rite*, it is a prescient work. As in the *Rite*, the ancient and modern coexist, seductively, tragically. 'Part of the fascination of the [Art Deco] style', write the design historians Charlotte and Tim Benton, 'lies precisely in its confrontation of new values with old, and in the hint of fragility and tragedy that often lurks behind its glitter.'[14] This modernism, associated with youthful decadence, often also carried with it a melancholic sense of loss, a feeling that is captured poignantly in

F. Scott Fitzgerald's landmark novel of the later Jazz Age, *The Great Gatsby* (1925). The exhilarating dance of modernity in the interwar years (mass culture, new technologies, social progress, an urgent desire to reinvent) masked the losses of the war. One can sense this in the Art Deco style.

Reaction to the revolutionary modern building of the Perret brothers was as divided as was the critics' response to the revolutionary ballet by Stravinsky and Nijinsky that was performed inside it. Indeed, much has been made of the striking aesthetic correspondences between theatre and ballet. Yet while it is true that the building's facade, the score and the choreography all triumphantly turned their backs on the immediate past, and while it is clear that both the *Rite* and the theatre prioritized structure over emotion, there are also important differences. The folklorism of the ballet in all its aspects represented the triumph of the Russian neo-nationalism of the Ballets Russes. The work of Auguste Perret, by contrast, initiated an essentially international modern classicism that would flourish after the War. (In its austerity it was accused at the time of not being French enough, greeted in certain quarters of the French press as '*une architecture boche*', '*du pur munichois*' – 'Kraut architecture', 'pure Munich style'.) It is only in his post-war works inspired by classical antiquity that one sees Stravinsky embracing more extensively the aesthetic ideals so evident in the Théâtre des Champs-Élysées. That said, even at the time of its premiere performances, a handful of critics detected something latently 'neoclassical' in the *Rite*: Jacques Rivière wrote of its 'clarity, simplicity, precision', while Vyacheslav Karatïgin noted 'a gravitation towards classical clarity and elegance'.[15] It is as if the critics sensed in the *Rite* a facet of Stravinsky's work that he was yet to realize for himself.

Stravinsky was later closely associated with another Perret building with a still more severe neoclassical exterior. The Salle Alfred-Cortot was completed in 1928, and was built within the

École Normale de Musique to which Stravinsky was appointed
co-professor of composition with Nadia Boulanger in 1935. The
interior is far less decorated than the Champs-Élysées, though it
still possesses a certain lyricism in its simple use of wood and
bronze-treated concrete. 'Living architecture', Perret once wrote,
'is that which faithfully expresses its own time.' The auditorium of
the Salle Alfred-Cortot achieved this by embracing the classical ideal.
No doubt Stravinsky would have been sensitive to how close this
came to his own aesthetic position in the 1920s and '30s. Another
exemplary building of the Art Deco style is the Salle Pleyel, designed
by the Pleyel company's director, Gustave Lyon. It opened on
18 October 1927 with a concert at which Stravinsky conducted
his own *Firebird* suite. Stravinsky's long-standing association
with Pleyel meant that he made regular appearances at this venue.
Here as soloist he premiered his *Capriccio* in 1929, conducted by
Ansermet. He had already given his Piano Concerto in the hall
under Bruno Walter and had conducted *The Rite of Spring* (a work
by this time 'reinvented' as a constructivist concert piece, in
keeping with its surroundings, rather than as primitive Russian
ritual). Even after he had emigrated to America, he kept returning
to the hall, most notably in 1957 to conduct one of his most
severely classical works: *Agon*. It is fascinating that he was so
closely linked to this monumental Art Deco building – simple,
classical, white inside and out – at just the time he was completing
Apollon musagète, his self-styed *ballet blanc*. Yet, ironically, it would
seem that Stravinsky was not enamoured with the space: in a letter
to Ansermet in 1928 he refers to the Salle Pleyel as 'ugly'. Of course,
Stravinsky's work was itself not immune from such judgements,
most famously the observation of Olin Downes, critic of the *New
York Times*, that Stravinsky's music was 'empty of the impulse of
beauty and feeling'.[16] But whatever Stravinsky himself felt, there
is a kinship between the modernism of much of his music of the
interwar years, and the new buildings in which they were heard.

More broadly, Paris after the war asserted itself as the capital of Western civilization.[17] Stravinsky would not have wished to be anywhere else, and he moved in the most extraordinary circles. The catalogue of his correspondence reveals a roll-call of the most important artistic figures of the interwar years, from Braque to Matisse to Poulenc to Valéry. One particular gathering of the leading artistic lights of the city has taken on almost legendary status. On 18 May 1922, at the luxurious Hôtel Majestic on avenue Kléber, following the premiere of *Renard* given by the Ballets Russes at the Opéra, Stravinsky sat down for dinner with Proust, Joyce, Picasso and Diaghilev. The hosts were the wealthy British writer Sydney Schiff and his wife, Violet. Richard Davenport-Hines goes so far as to claim that the gathering came to represent the high point of European modernism, and one of Paris's defining moments as a cultural capital. Stravinsky and his fellow guests were in 1922 'reckoned by intelligent Parisians to be more important than politicians or manufacturers'.[18] Like all such gatherings, the fact of its taking place is probably more significant than the ideas that were exchanged between the guests. Such immense egos were hardly likely to have interacted easily, and in any case the wine was flowing freely. Proust apparently proposed to Stravinsky his admiration for late Beethoven, to which Stravinsky is alleged to have retorted, 'I detest Beethoven.' But as a symbol of Paris as a crucible of new art in the 1920s, this dinner cannot be matched.

Since the spectacular Paris premiere of *The Rite of Spring* in 1913 and the politer reception a year later of *The Nightingale* at the Opéra, Stravinsky and his music had all but vanished from the Paris scene. The economies of exile in Switzerland during the war years along with the disruption to the activities of the Ballets Russes had necessitated a concentration on smaller-scale projects. For nearly three years Stravinsky had not set foot in Paris. But on

Igor and Catherine Stravinsky, 1928.

15 May 1920, back once more on the stage of the Opéra, he was
relaunched into the limelight with the premiere by the Ballets
Russes of *Pulcinella*, conducted by Ansermet, with scenario and
choreography by Massine and designs by Picasso. Both the public
and the critics loved it. In an interview published on the day of the
premiere, Stravinsky himself claimed that it represented 'a new

kind of music'. Forty years later, in his conversations with Robert Craft, Stravinsky would suggest that the critics had not understood the work, that he had been 'blamed for deserting modernism"', that he had acted sacrilegiously towards his musical models. But in fact *Pulcinella* received general acclaim: the vast majority of critics recognized a modernism appropriate to the changed post-war world, a shift in priorities towards a new simplicity. In short, *Pulcinella* was received as chic. It was comic, youthful, eclectic, playful and ironic, possessing *surprise et nouveauté* at every turn, with a simplicity of melody and vitality of rhythm, and a presentation of a modernized classical music that resonated with the post-war *rappel à l'ordre*. In the way in which it looked both backwards and forwards simultaneously, it echoed precisely the aesthetic of Art Deco.

The impulse for *Pulcinella* came from Diaghilev, who had formulated the idea of the ballet on encountering *commedia dell'arte* puppet theatre while touring southern Italy with Massine. All Diaghilev wanted on this occasion was arrangements of some music by the eighteenth-century Italian composer Giovanni Battista Pergolesi (though it later turned out that the music was not just by Pergolesi but also by a number of his contemporaries). Manuel de Falla had been his first choice to make the arrangements, but Falla was busy on other projects. Diaghilev turned to Stravinsky, who was nonplussed at the suggestion. Diaghilev persuaded him at least to consult the transcriptions of the music Diaghilev had himself made both in Naples and at the British Museum, and Stravinsky was instantly smitten. 'I looked, and I fell in love', he later recalled. He set to work immediately.

At its premiere *Pulcinella* was billed simply as 'music by Pergolesi, arranged and orchestrated by Igor Stravinsky'. Yet it has subsequently come to be identified more directly with Stravinsky as composer rather than arranger, in part as a consequence of the various concert suites he made of the score.

While he later asserted that the 'remarkable thing about *Pulcinella* is not how much but how little has been added or changed', the alterations are significant enough to turn the music into something unmistakably of its own time. Stravinsky began by working directly onto the transcriptions Diaghilev had given him, subtly annotating the melodies and bass lines of arias by Pergolesi, trio sonata movements by Gallo, a tarantella by Wassenaer. Sometimes the result was just a representation of the original in Stravinsky's own accent. No one could mistake the witty trombone and double-bass melody of the 'Vivo' for anything other than Stravinsky, even though every note of Pergolesi's music is still present. There are cunning harmonic touches, anachronistic pedal points and off-beat accents that reveal the thumbprint of the arranger, but it remains a loving, albeit humorous, homage to Pergolesi. Elsewhere, however, Stravinsky declares his hand more decisively. In the 'Serenata', for instance, he adds an unchanging drone, which denies the music its forward movement and whose resulting dissonances bestow a languid, melancholic air. The 'Finale' is radically recomposed, repeating bars, moving them around, adding new harmonies and shifting downbeats, resulting in a rhythmically energized music that is categorically Stravinskian and, one might say, almost as Russian in spirit as it is Italian.

Stravinsky's Russian manner notwithstanding, *Pulcinella* represents his decisive turn towards the West. He understood that. He later described *Pulcinella* as 'the epiphany through which the whole of my late work became possible. It was a backward look, of course – the first of many love affairs in that direction – but it was a look in the mirror, too.' In its overt dependence on the music of the past, *Pulcinella* represented a crucial moment in Stravinsky's artistic development. Just as, after the First World War, Picasso had felt the need to seek a rapprochement with the traditional forms of art he had once rejected so that he could move forward, equally *Pulcinella* revealed to Stravinsky the possibilities of an engagement with all kinds of earlier music in order to renew his own musical language. Over the coming decades he would take his material from wherever he found it: Monteverdi, Bach, Mozart, Beethoven, Verdi, Glinka, Tchaikovsky, jazz. He would describe himself as suffering from a 'rare form of kleptomania'. But what was crucial was not the material itself but his attitude to it. Everything he touched he made his own. It is in this sense that Asaf'yev memorably described Stravinsky as 'the Pushkin of Russian music'. Like the eclectic allusions of Art Deco, the past in Stravinsky was reordered and turned to distinctively modern purposes, 'obedient to the tempi and rhythm of contemporary life'.[19]

And yet, while Stravinsky swiftly became the chic, cosmopolitan composer, speaking the international language of modern Western music, the borrowings here speak of something else. As a Russian confronting Pergolesi in this way, he was brought up hard against his own exile. Displaced and misplaced: the sense of irony in *Pulcinella* is strong. The closer Stravinsky moved to the Western classical style, the more acute became the sense of his distance from it. The fragmentation of the 'Finale', denying the source music its conventional way of speaking, is a sign of this. Like the costumes in Picasso's original production, Stravinsky wore the music of Pergolesi, Gallo and the rest as masks. The novelist and essayist Milan Kundera, himself a long-time émigré from the Communist regime in his native Czechoslovakia, understood all too well why Stravinsky had developed such a relationship with the Western tradition:

Without a doubt, Stravinsky, like all the others, bore with him the wound of his emigration; without a doubt, his artistic evolution would have taken a different path if he had been able to stay where he was born. In fact, the start of his journey through the history of music coincides roughly with the moment when his native country ceases to exist for him; having understood that no country could replace it, he finds his only homeland in music; this is not just a nice lyrical conceit of mine, I think it in an absolutely concrete way: his only home was music, all of music by all musicians, the very history of music; there he decided to establish himself, to take root, to live; there he ultimately found his only compatriots, his only intimates, his only neighbors, from Pérotin to Webern; it is with them that he began a long conversation, which ended only with his death . . .

His detractors, the defenders of music conceived as expression of feelings, who grew irate at his unbearably discreet 'affective activity' and accused him of 'poverty of heart', didn't have heart enough themselves to understand the wounded feelings that lay behind his vagabondage through the history of music.[20]

When Peter the Great decided to start afresh in the marshlands of northwest Russia and to found a new city for a new kind of empire, he borrowed Italians such as the Naples-born Carlo Rossi as the architect of so many of the beautiful classical buildings in the place that took his name. When Igor Stravinsky decided to start afresh after the austere wartime years and adopt a new musical style for a new age, he borrowed Italians such as Giovanni Battista Pergolesi, who flourished in Naples, as the source of his beautiful classical music. While it would be foolish to make any simple connection between Stravinsky's childhood biography and his compositional work in exile, there remains a lingering suspicion, as articulated so poetically by Kundera, that the origins of Stravinsky's vagabondage through European classicism in the name of chic can be found in the Europeanized Russia of his youth.

Across many decades, commentators have taken *Pulcinella* as marking the beginning of Stravinsky's neoclassical style.

Neoclassicism came to stand – as it still does – for an entire 30-year period of Stravinsky's output. Yet the term embraces such a wide range of music and ideas that its explanatory power would seem limited. It is often used to refer to a music that looks back to – even pastiches – the eighteenth century, a so-called 'Back to Bach' movement. But such a description could, at best, be relevant to only a small handful of the more than 50 works Stravinsky produced between 1920 and 1950. Pastiche, too, was only rarely essayed – *Mavra* (1922) and *The Fairy's Kiss* (1928) being the obvious examples – and even then not without a critical aspect. On the other hand, if the notion of the neoclassical is more broadly understood to embrace eclecticism as well as a rethinking of antiquity in the manner of Art Deco, then this comes closer to the spirit of some of Stravinsky's interwar activities. Yet the borrowing and reconfiguration of musical *objets trouvés* encountered in *Pulcinella* had already been a facet of his pre-war works, pre-eminently *Petrushka*; they would remain features of his music after 1950. So even in this sense the term 'neoclassical' is, at best, only crudely able to define a style, a practice or even a period.

In fact, the word 'neoclassicism' was not applied to Stravinsky's music until 1923, in a review by the Russian émigré critic Boris de Schloezer in response to a work that, at first hearing, could not be more different from *Pulcinella*: the *Symphonies of Wind Instruments*. Scott Messing's extensive investigation into the history of the term 'neoclassicism' in music has shown how Schloezer helped shift the meaning of *néoclassicisme* away from its hitherto pejorative associations with late nineteenth-century German instrumental music and towards the greater simplicity and objectivity espoused by the anti-Romantic post-war Paris avant-garde. This is made abundantly clear in Schloezer's review, in which he presents Stravinsky as the antipode of a Teutonic expressionist aesthetic. 'Stravinsky is the most anti-Wagnerian of musicians; he realizes the most forceful reaction against "Tristan" which has ever been accomplished.' The sense of the neoclassical in the *Symphonies of Wind Instruments*, then, has nothing to do with direct allusions to earlier music (there are none) and everything to do with its relative simplicity, objectivity and purity.

> This genial work is only a system of sounds, which follow one another and group themselves according to purely musical affinities . . . Emotions, feelings, desires, aspirations – this is the terrain from which he has pushed his work. The art of Stravinsky is nevertheless strongly expressive; he moves us profoundly and his perception is never formularized; but there is one specific emotion, a musical emotion; but it retains grace infallibly by its force and its perfection.
>
> In the face of the neo-romanticism of Schoenberg, Stravinsky reestablishes the ancient classical, pre-Beethoven tradition.[21]

In this context it is perfectly possible to see how the innovative structure of the *Symphonies* is in tune with the reinvention of the classical found in the work of Perret and his Art Deco contemporaries.

Pulcinella was the last work Stravinsky wrote at Morges. The family move to Carantec in Brittany that took place in the summer of 1920 marked the start of Stravinsky's long sojourn in France (his 'second motherland'), and it was there that he began the *Symphonies of Wind Instruments*. It was finished in the glamorous Art Nouveau surroundings of Garches. It is fascinating that *Pulcinella* and the *Symphonies*, two works that sound poles apart, were written so close to each other at this important turning point in Stravinsky's life. They show us the two sides of the new post-war Stravinskian coin. While *Pulcinella* was undoubtedly chic, the *Symphonies of Wind Instruments* was, on Stravinsky's own admission, 'devoid of all the elements which infallibly appeal to the ordinary listener . . . not meant "to please" an audience'. This is a typically

Stravinskian a posteriori justification of the less than satisfactory premiere performance in London in 1921, under the direction of Sergey Koussevitzky, which elicited laughter and hissing. Yet there is no denying that the *Symphonies* is a sombre work, an austere ritual, betraying its origins *à la mémoire de Claude Debussy*.

It began as a very simple, chordal piano composition, commissioned to appear alongside other short Debussy tributes in a commemorative supplement to *La Revue musicale*, and was composed in a single day in June 1920. It has the character of a chorale that, conventionally, might appear at the end of a liturgical work: the bass line circles round itself, eventually coming to rest on a low C, above which Stravinsky constructs a beautifully spaced chord that seems to resonate out into eternity. Though audibly a point of arrival, the intersecting C-major and G-major triads also lend the final chord a strangely unresolved, melancholic tone. Such an instrumental chorale as a gesture of closure was to become a regular feature of Stravinsky's music, right down to his final major work, the *Requiem Canticles*, and had already been suggested in the monumental chords that close *The Firebird* (later renamed by Stravinsky as 'Hymn'). So when Stravinsky decided to draw this material into a larger work for wind instruments it was inevitable that this would form its ending and he would need to compose backwards from it, cutting and pasting ideas as he went, as if making a kind of Cubist collage. For example, as he explained to Craft, a few days after completing the first draft 'two adumbrative bits of chorale [were added] to the body of the piece' in order to give the impression that the chorale belonged in some way to the rest of the work. Perhaps as a consequence of these unusual circumstances, the work that emerged was, in formal terms, the most innovative Stravinsky ever produced, and remains one of the most radical and influential structures of the first half of the twentieth century.

The mosaic-like structure of the *Symphonies* had its precedents, most notably in the opening tableau of *Petrushka*, but here Stravinsky pushes to extremes the juxtaposition and non-sequential repetition of strongly contrasting blocks of music. As distinct from the case in *Petrushka*, the organization of these blocks cannot immediately be accounted for with reference to any explicit scenario or programme. It appears as an entirely 'abstract' piece of music, a 'system of sounds', in Schloezer's words. In its non-organic manner of composition, in its non-developmental, anti-symphonic structure (despite its title, which is merely meant to signify a 'sounding together') and even in the absence of expression, it clearly sets itself up as an anti-Romantic statement. In that the work celebrates discontinuity over connectedness, it has become the paradigm for a particular strand of abstract modernism for subsequent generations of composers.

Neoclassicism in Stravinsky, then, is not concerned with a simple borrowing from the past, though allusions to music and practices of other eras and traditions can form an important part of it. Neither does Stravinsky's neoclassicism represent, as his critics would have it, an abandonment of modernism. (Schoenberg mocked Stravinsky in the 1920s as a mere '*kleiner Modernsky*'; Schoenberg's champion Adorno wrote in the 1940s of Stravinsky's 'regression to tonality'.) In fact, the objectivizing, formalizing and distancing processes of Stravinsky's music in the 1920s aligned themselves far more closely with similar tendencies in Schoenberg's twelve-note music than either composer was willing to admit, as contemporary references to Schoenberg as a 'neoclassicist' make clear.

Precision, simplicity, clarity, order, gracefulness: these are the defining traits of Stravinsky's neoclassical style. Stravinsky chooses to construct and interpret his contemporary world through the classical past, that is, by means of an idealized view of both antiquity and the music of the seventeenth and eighteenth centuries. In so doing, Stravinsky's neoclassical music celebrates joyfully the aesthetics of Paris Art Deco: 'composition and *haute couture* collided in the name of modernism', as Davis puts it.[22] But equally

Stravinsky's neoclassical music, in all its many guises, is capable of expressing a deeper sense of loss, of a distance from the very past that is being embraced. Both the lamenting chorale of the *Symphonies of Wind Instruments* and the fragmented Gallo of the 'Finale' of *Pulcinella* speak in different ways of dislocation and exile. Stravinsky's neoclassical music articulates alienation, the hallmark of modernism.

There are, however, other ways of reading the *Symphonies of Wind Instruments* besides Schloezer's structuralist one. Many early commentators picked up on the Russianness of its melodic materials. Stravinsky's account in the *Autobiography* of this 'austere ceremony' – 'short litanies', 'cantilena', 'liturgical dialogue, 'soft chanting [*psalmodiant*]' – hints at a religious underpinning in keeping with the work's origins as a *tombeau*. Taruskin has shown how the structure of the work can be mapped convincingly onto the organization of the *panikhida* or Orthodox office of the dead, replete with opening calls of 'Alleluia', ritual recitations and strophic hymns. Further, for Taruskin, the *Symphonies* is the culmination of Stravinsky's *drobnost'*, a word he appropriates to indicate the inherent Russianness of the 'splintered' aspects of the musical form. The *Symphonies of Wind Instruments*, then, is a work on the cusp, as much an epiphany as its near-contemporary *Pulcinella*. It is turned resolutely to the future, yet its fractured, modernist surfaces echo a Russian past. This contradiction is captured in the music's poignantly melancholic character. Is it going too far to propose that the laments of the *Symphonies* are not just for Stravinsky's great friend Debussy, but for himself, for his lost Russia?

6

To the Glory of God

Nice, 11 October 1925. Stravinsky is sitting at his desk, writing a letter to the poet, dramatist, artist and film-maker Jean Cocteau, his friend and neighbour. 'My dear Jean,' he begins:

> for some time now I have been haunted by the idea of
> composing an opera in Latin on the subject of a tragedy from
> the ancient world with which everyone would be familiar.
> I should like to entrust to you the verbal realization of this work,
> as I proposed to you the other day. The scenario as well as the
> staging would be realized through our intimate collaboration.

And then, in typical fashion, before even a word or note of the work has been composed, he raises the matter of the division of authors' rights, just to be sure that, in the event of the failure of the project, Cocteau is left in no doubt about who owns the idea. Stravinsky is never one to allow friendship to get in the way of money.

He is after a libretto, he says, that must be entirely banal, intended for a large public who will need to understand nothing of what is represented but who, rather, will simply see the movements on the stage. Cocteau has already completed the first version by 28 October, but it is not to Stravinsky's liking. 'That's not banal,' says Stravinsky when he meets Cocteau, 'that's Wagnerian. I need a much simpler libretto, a libretto for everybody. Nobody can understand Wagnerian librettos, not even Wagner.' '*Pas d'inquiétude*', replies Cocteau, '*Je vais faire un autre*' – 'Don't worry. I shall do another one.' And so he sets to work on a second version, which he sends to Stravinsky. 'This is still Wagnerian', Stravinsky tells Cocteau. Through gritted teeth, Cocteau takes the criticism. 'My dear,' he says, 'it's a pleasure to work with you! I shall make a third libretto.' And so he does. And this time the result pleases Stravinsky greatly, because it is much more like the libretto for an Italian opera. 'That's what I need!' smiles Stravinsky.

The friendship between Stravinsky and Cocteau had extended back to the early years of their association with the Ballets Russes, but it had hit choppy waters after the publication in 1918 of Cocteau's *Le Coq et l'arlequin*, his French nationalist manifesto that rejected Russian and German music, lumped Stravinsky together with Wagner and Debussy as 'first-rate octopuses', and proposed Satie's simplicity, his 'music of everyday life', as the model for the music of the future. A reconciliation was eventually forged on the back of Cocteau's positive defence of *Mavra* in an issue of *Vanity Fair* in 1922. This short *opera buffa*, to a libretto by Boris Kochno after Pushkin's story 'The Little House at Kolomna', dedicated '*à la mémoire de Pouchkine, Glinka et Tschaïkovsky*', had not been well received at its staged premiere at the Paris Opéra. Stravinsky later recounted the damning verdict of Otto Kahn, the wealthy German-American patron of the arts who was to have taken the Ballets Russes to the USA: 'I liked it all, then "poop" it ends too quickly.' The critics, for the most part, condemned its apparent change in style, its pastiche, its unamusing *plaisanterie musicale*. For Cocteau, Satie and the composers of the group nicknamed Les Six whom they inspired (Milhaud and Poulenc among them), however, it represented a definitive turn towards the anti-Romantic fold to which so many of the youth of post-war Paris now belonged. In August 1922 Stravinsky told Ansermet that 'Cocteau writes to me frequently; now we are

Jean Cocteau, Pablo Picasso, Igor Stravinsky and Olga Picasso, Juan-les-Pins, 1925.

friends.' In December he attended the premiere of Cocteau's version of Sophocles' *Antigone* at the Théâtre de l'Atelier in Paris, with music by Arthur Honneger, sets by Picasso and costumes by Chanel. It made a strong impression. And when in September 1925 Cocteau read to him his tragicomic play *Orphée*, Stravinsky was so impressed that within a month they were working together on *Oedipus Rex*.

> *Spectateurs, vous allez entendre une version latine d'Oedipe-Roi . . .*
> Ladies and gentlemen, you are about to hear a Latin version of King Oedipus. This version is an opera-oratorio; based on the tragedy of Sophocles, but preserving only a certain monumental aspect of its various scenes. And so (wishing to spare your ears and your memories) I shall recall the story as we go along.

Stravinsky and Cocteau cheer the success of *Oedipus Rex* in 1952.

These are the first words of the Prologue, spoken by the Narrator in the French of Cocteau (if the audience is predominantly francophone) or else in a suitable translation into the vernacular of the audience (such as the English version by E. E. Cummings). The text needs to be delivered, Stravinsky tells us, with a detached voice, 'like a *conférencier*'. This narrator is not new in Stravinsky's work: he had already been present in *The Soldier's Tale*. Here the role achieves the monumentality Stravinsky and Cocteau so desired for their 'still-life': a formal, stylized work, like the operas and oratorios of Handel and not at all like the music dramas of Wagner. What the audience witnesses is not the tragedy of Oedipus but rather a retelling of the story of Oedipus. The Narrator tells what is going to happen before it actually happens. He stands outside the drama, providing a frame for it, like the entry and exit music in *Renard*, making it clear to the spectators that what they are experiencing is a piece of theatre, from which they remain detached. It is not real life.

In any case, real life in twentieth-century France did not generally take place in Latin, which is the language in which the soloists and chorus sing. Stravinsky's letter to Cocteau makes it clear that the Latin language was a part of the work from its conception. Cocteau's French text was translated into Latin by a Sorbonne theology student (and eventual cardinal) named Jean Daniélou. Ancient Greek would have been more authentic to Sophocles, but Stravinsky wanted a language that would have been reasonably familiar to his audience in that it was still in use in ritual contexts, primarily in the Catholic Church. 'Latin is a language that's not dead but turned to stone', he later commented. The use of Latin both ritualizes the drama and distances the audience from it. Since Latin had no living spoken tradition, it also meant that Stravinsky could approach the texts merely as so much phonetic material with which he could play freely, as if they were just more *pribaoutki*, thereby separating music and text, music and meaning, and creating a further distancing effect. The shifting accentuation of the name 'Oedipus' sung in the opening chorus is a case in point. Opprobrium came from the pens of critics who did not recognize what Stravinsky was doing, and who did not hear the rhythmic dynamism that this practice lends the music.

Though the premiere in Paris of *Oedipus Rex* on 30 May 1927 was a concert performance, Cocteau and Stravinsky had all along planned for the work to be staged (which it was, nine months later, in Vienna), where the decor, costumes and style of acting would add to the stylization of the drama. It was intended that the characters should be masked, moving only their arms and heads, giving the impression of living statues. The original idea was for the chorus to be 'concealed behind a kind of bas-relief' representing sculptured drapery and revealing only the faces of the singers. And the Narrator was to have been in evening dress, acting as an intermediary between stage and auditorium. All this was very much in keeping with ideas of anti-realism in the theatre that were circulating in the first decades of the twentieth century, with which Cocteau certainly was familiar. Parallels can be identified with, in particular, the work with masks, puppets and pantomime of the Russian director Vsevolod Meyerhold; or with Bertolt Brecht, whose theory of epic theatre was being developed at this time in the spirit of the Neue Sachlichkeit (New Objectivity) of Weimar Germany, which aimed by means of alienation (*Verfremdung*) to keep the audience at a critical distance; or with the work of the Russian film-maker Sergey Eisenstein, who had been a designer for Meyerhold, who was coming to prominence in the late 1920s with *Battleship Potemkin* (1925) and *October* (1928) and who believed, like Brecht, that his art should be didactic and incite the viewer to action; or with the 'theatre of cruelty' being developed by Antonin Artaud, which also rejected realistic narrative. Stravinsky later said of *Oedipus* that 'My audience is not indifferent to the fate of the person, but I think it far more concerned with the person of the fate, and the delineation of it which can be achieved uniquely in music.' In other words, because the 'universal' story was well known, and because it was presented in a monumental manner, the attention of the audience would be focused on the *musical* drama.

Oedipus also invites comparison, once again, with the world of Art Deco in which both Stravinsky and Cocteau were moving, whose reach was at its most extensive at this time in the wake of the 1925 Paris Exhibition. The monumentality of the achievements of Art Deco architecture finds its counterpart in *Oedipus Rex*. Just as Art Deco buildings borrowed from antiquity, stripped to their essential details, in order to celebrate the modern world, so *Oedipus Rex* takes a Greek myth, as narrated by an ancient author, and retells the tragedy for the post-war age. Stravinsky's musical borrowings are fundamental to the way in which the work speaks; it is one of his most eclectic works to date, recognized in his description of it as a '*Merzbild*', a word appropriated from the Dadaist artist Kurt Schwitters and suggesting a collage made from discarded everyday objects. The juxtaposition of styles adds to the dimension of alienation and distancing that the work achieves. As befits an oratorio, Handel (by way of Gluck) is present at the start, in the chorus that both participates in and comments on the drama. Creon's aria borrows formulae from Handel, which lend the music a further monumentality. Here the simplest 'everyday' musical object, a descending C-major arpeggio, is worked in a decidedly un-Handelian manner. Jocasta's Act Two recitative and aria take liberally from Verdi, but Verdi at a distance, a borrowed Verdian operatic monumentality, Verdi as seen through a Stravinskian prism. Oedipus' first entry in Act One, 'Liberi, vos liberabo a peste', also has something of nineteenth-century *bel canto* about it, though its incantatory quality shares as much with the sound of Russian Orthodox chanting, while the wind accompaniment imitates a Baroque dotted figure. Neither Oedipus nor Jocasta is without emotion, but the audience remains alienated as a consequence of their musical representation.

What, ultimately, is *Oedipus Rex* 'about', if it is not concerned with plot or emotion? Early in its history Boris Asaf'yev claimed that 'the music of *Oedipus* is timely – a strong plea for humanity and the ideas of humanism scorned by contemporary European civilization.'[1] Others have invited examination of its treatment of the theme of human fate in the context of the dramatic rituals that preceded it, most particularly *The Rite of Spring*, *Les Noces* and *The Soldier's Tale*. But it is a dangerous fate indeed that unfolds with such inevitability, and whose course is impossible to alter. This was made clear in Cocteau's later reworking of the Oedipus story into a play under the revelatory title *La Machine infernale*,

premiered in 1934 in the Théâtre des Champs-Élysées. The ending
of *Oedipus Rex* may not be so explicitly violent as the ending of the
Rite, but the onlooker is powerless all the same to intercede, caught
up in the infernal machine of the relentless, infinitely repeating
ostinato (the 'fate' motif) that closes the work.

It might therefore seem surprising to think of *Oedipus Rex*
as a religious work. It had been prompted in the first place by an
account of the life of St Francis discovered by chance at a railway
station bookstall. In July 1926, in the midst of his work on the
opera-oratorio, Stravinsky broke off to write his first ever sacred
piece, a setting of *Otche nash*, the Slavonic text of the *Pater noster*,
intended for liturgical use. On 6 April 1926 he had written to
Diaghilev from Nice:

> I have not been a Communicant in twenty years, and it is
> because of an extreme spiritual need that I am going to take
> communion now. In the next days I will go to Confession, and
> before the Confession, I want, as far as is possible, to ask the
> forgiveness of everyone. I ask this of you also, dear Serge . . .
> to forgive me the transgressions of all these years that have
> passed without repentance before God . . .

Living among a large émigré community and a stone's throw
from the Russian church in Nice, with the beleaguered Catherine
increasingly seeking consolation in her faith, Stravinsky's spiritual
renewal at this time should perhaps not appear so unexpected.
The paraphernalia of the Orthodox Church – crosses, icons,
observation of saints' days – had always been part of his life. The
forgiveness he sought may have been born in part of the guilt he
felt for his double life with Vera. But the influence of Cocteau was
also crucial. Cocteau had himself returned to the sacraments of the
Catholic Church in 1925. He, in turn, had come under the influence
of the neo-Thomist philosopher and professor at the Institut

Catholique Jacques Maritain, whose *Art et scolastique* of 1919 had quoted, approvingly, from *Le Coq et l'arlequin*, and which resulted in Cocteau's *Lettre à Jacques Maritain* (1926), a shameless piece of self-justification and public self-reinvention that put even Stravinsky's efforts of this kind into the shade. In *Art et scolastique* Maritain proposed a return to the medieval idea of the artist as artisan, very much in tune with the new aesthetic sensibilities of post-war France, where the ideas of craft, rule and form held sway. This was a call to divine order, or to take the title of another of Cocteau's works from 1926, *Le Rappel à l'ordre*. Art was to be autonomous, art for art's sake, in a fascinating distant echo of the rallying cry of *Mir iskusstva*. The classical was elevated to the highest level. Art leads to the good and therefore to the spirit.

Maritain's manifesto for a modern art built out of a nostalgia for a pre-Romantic age clearly hit home with Stravinsky. He had read Maritain in the early 1920s, though the two (in the company of Vera and Arthur Lourié) did not meet until 1926. The Russian émigré composer Lourié, who was Stravinsky's assistant and official spokesman between 1925 and 1930, was an important conduit for these ideas. So was another Russian émigré, Pierre Souvtchinksy (Pyotr Suvchinsky), whom Stravinsky first met in Berlin in 1922 and who made the connection between the emergent ideology of Eurasianism and Stravinsky's music, which he read as transcending the (human) subjective experience of time in order to reach a more 'real' spiritual level. He might well have been thinking of the ending of *Oedipus Rex*. Indeed, Lourié's essay on that work from 1927 was strongly guided by Souvtchinsky and echoes the neo-Thomist aesthetic position: 'The significance of *Oedipus* consists in the naked expression of truth and purity, and everything is sacrificed to this expression.' Such views, though, were already to be found in Stravinsky's essay from 1924 on his *Octet*; they run right through his *Autobiography* ghosted by Nouvel and first published in French in 1935; and they are fundamental to the *Poetics of Music*, ghosted by Roland-Manuel (Roland Alexis Manuel Lévy) but deeply indebted to the thinking of Souvtchinsky.

> My Octuor is not an 'emotive' work but a musical composition based on objective elements which are sufficient in themselves. ('Some Ideas about my Octuor')

> music is, by its very nature, essentially powerless to *express* anything at all . . . (*An Autobiography*)

> Jacques Maritain reminds us that in the mighty structure of medieval civilization, the artist held only the rank of an artisan . . . Do we not, in truth, ask the impossible of music when we expect it to express feelings, to translate dramatic situations, even to imitate nature? (*Poetics of Music*)

Lourié's first article on Stravinsky, published in 1925, was a short study of the Sonata for Piano (1924). It lauds the work for its rupture with the romantic sonata that had reached its decadent apogee in the hands of Skryabin and Debussy. In going 'Back to Bach', Stravinsky was returning to the primacy of objective, musical form and the principles of artisanship. The model of Bach for this work cannot be ignored; Bach was adopted as a symbol for both craft and purity. Purity, too, is the catchword for *Apollo*, Stravinsky's next work after *Oedipus Rex*. In reviewing the work, Boris de Schloezer wrote of its 'serenity' and 'purity', with all the holy implications these words carry – so much so, in fact, that he rashly predicted Stravinsky's next work would be a Mass.

Stravinsky did not write his Mass until 1948. But the next major work after *Apollo* to employ voices might as well have been a Mass. The *Symphony of Psalms* was composed 'à la gloire de DIEU', as the score's frontispiece proclaims. It was commissioned as an 'abstract' symphony by Sergey Koussevitsky for the Boston Symphony

Orchestra's fiftieth birthday, but from the moment he started composing it was clear that Stravinsky had a sacred piece in mind. The outer movements are in fact dedicated to specific church festivals and, as a whole, it became an act of renewal of faith, a personal testimony on the part of someone returning to the body of the Church after a long absence. Indeed, the psalm excerpts selected for the first two movements offer a very personal supplication: 'Exaudi orationem meam, Domine' ('Hear my prayer, O Lord, and give ear unto my cry', from Psalm 39) and 'Expectans expectavi Dominum' ('I waited patiently for the Lord: and he inclined to me and heard my cry', from Psalm 40). The final movement is a setting in its entirety of Psalm 150, the 'musician's psalm': 'Alleluia, Laudate Dominum' ('Alleluia, praise ye the Lord . . . Praise him with the sound of the trumpet . . .').

A clue to the significance of the work for Stravinsky is perhaps to be found in one of the lines he chooses to set in the first movement: '*quoniam advena ego sum apud te*' ('for I am a stranger with Thee'), a stranger to God having drifted from the Church. In the standard French translation, which Stravinsky would surely also have known, there are even stronger personal resonances: '*car je suis un étranger chez toi, un voyageur*', 'a foreigner . . . a nomad' – words that would have spoken personally to the émigré composer, always on the move, still not settled in one place. Stravinsky's biographer Stephen Walsh suggests that the *Psalms* come 'closer to the soul of Stravinsky's art than any work of his since the *Symphonies of Wind Instruments*',[2] and Stravinsky recalled that the first movement 'was composed in a state of religious and musical ebullience'. Yet, despite all this, despite even the exceptionally rare use near the start of the marking *espressivo* – an impassioned rising and falling semitone figure on horn and cello, later picked up by the choir as their opening exhortation – the work does not express these feelings directly; rather, like *Oedipus Rex*, it is a monumental, ritual statement. Also as in *Oedipus* before it, the use of the 'petrified'

Latin language immediately distances, depersonalizes, as well as imbuing the work with a ceremonial quality. It is presented as a collective, not an individual plea. The text at the start is not repeated by the chorus – it is set straight through – but there is a high degree of repetition in the music, simple repeating melodic figures, ostinatos or mobiles using a motoric semiquaver rhythm, pedal points, that give the music a static character. This becomes exaggerated towards the end of the final movement in the ecstatic, slow tread of a basic ostinato bass line that continues seemingly endlessly: it has, in Walsh's words, a 'sublime monotony'. The famous opening E-minor chord with its distinctive spacing punctuates the course of the first movement, defining its ritual space like the pillars supporting a great medieval cathedral. Indeed, just a few years later, Stravinsky was to write in the *Autobiography* that one 'could not better define the sensation produced by music than by saying that it is identical with that evoked by contemplation of the interplay of architectural forms'. Between these pillars is to be found more 'architectural' material in the shape of arpeggio figures, first in the woodwind, then in the piano, which sound as if they could have been taken straight from a piano finger exercise manual. Like Stravinsky's treatment of the text as a kind of found object, the presence here of this neutral, abstract, non-expressive musical material reinforces the distancing effect, so that the listener's attention is directed not to the material itself but to what the composer does with it. Stravinsky, it should be remembered, always composed at the piano, and given that such pianistic studies would now have formed part of his daily practice routine as an active concert pianist, it should hardly be surprising that such material found its way into his music in all manner of different guises.[3]

With the absence of upper strings, the scoring distances itself from the expressive sound-world of German Romanticism, and instead points back to Russia with the bell-like sounds of wind and brass, piano and harp. The contrast with *Apollo* (1927–8), for strings alone, which had adopted a chic French poise, is especially striking, as Stravinsky now reconfigures aspects of his earlier Dionysian Russian self: at times it almost sounds as if he is reworking the *Symphonies of Wind Instruments*, right down to the repeated statements of 'Alleluia'. That he was 'thinking in Russian' during the composition of the *Psalms* is borne out by his claim that he had in fact begun working not in Latin but in ancient Slavonic, the '*Laudate dominum*' of Psalm 150 being initially '*Gospodi pomiluy*', 'a prayer to the Russian image of the infant Christ with orb and sceptre'. The idea of a collective faith expressed in the first movement, in parallel with the neo-Thomist thinking Stravinsky had found in Maritain, takes on a further anti-Romantic dimension in the second movement, where a neo-Baroque sense of craft and order is writ large in the form of a spectacular double fugue. (There is perhaps again a clue hidden in the chosen psalm fragment: '*Direxit gressus meos*', 'ordered my goings'.) Its four-note subject has strong echoes of one of the most famous fugue subjects of all, also in C minor, from Bach's *Musical Offering*. But this subject is not extended or directed in a Bachian manner; rather, it is woven into a much more static texture of motivic interplay. The certainty of the High Baroque is stripped away to suggest modern doubt. The final and longest movement begins quietly, radiantly, not in celebration, as one might expect of a Western setting of the word 'Alleluia' à la *Messiah*, but in the contemplative Russian manner: a recurring cadential progression that, in its final iteration, offers a glorious, understated, C-major image of transcendence. Just for a moment, this large collective ritual speaks with an unexpectedly personal voice. The émigré seems to have discovered his spiritual home.

Stravinsky's neoclassical style, claims Tamara Levitz in her revisionist account of the composer's modernism, was a consequence of his Orthodox faith. 'Ever since reconverting to that religion in 1926 Stravinsky had found that the Orthodox Church provided him with a metaphysical homeland of Christian dogma to replace the physical home he had lost.'[4] For Levitz, one work in particular speaks, complexly, of Stravinsky's return to faith: *Perséphone*, completed in 1934. Like *Oedipus Rex* it is, at the surface level, a presentation of a classical myth, a setting of André Gide's retelling of the seventh-century BC Homeric *Hymn to Demeter*. But, argues Levitz, it is ultimately an expression of Stravinsky's belief in divine revelation. This opens up the possibility, again, of a reading of a work beyond its ostensible narrative. It has profound implications, for example, for an understanding of the idiosyncratic text setting here: like his earlier 'rejoicing discovery', by working against the rhythms of Gide's text, Stravinsky could draw attention to the very sounds of syllables rather than the sense of words. This was an approach, as Souvtchinsky later argued, that aligned Stravinsky closely with the practices of Orthodox chanting, where an egoless state was achieved by the worshipper in focusing not on the meaning of what was being sung but on individual or reiterated syllables.[5] The simple, often static, diatonic harmony throughout *Perséphone*, and the pleasure taken in sound itself, creates a very different sense of time, a transcendent or 'divine' time, an 'ontological time', to use the phrase of Souvtchinsky that would reappear in the *Poetics of Music* he would draft for Stravinsky later in the 1930s. The result is, in Levitz's phrase, a 'sacred formalism' which places *Perséphone* very much in the same company as *Oedipus Rex* and the *Symphony of Psalms*.

For Craft, Russia haunts *Oedipus Rex*. The *Symphony of Psalms*, in Taruskin's view, demonstrates that 'Stravinsky the *ur*-Russian and the modernist was back'.[6] In 'Sur ce lit' from *Perséphone* Stravinsky ignored Gide's French versification entirely and confessed that he had originally written it to his own Russian words. The Latin opera-oratorio, the Latin church psalms and the classical French melodrama all ultimately speak of something other than the neoclassical formality that they purport to convey. Behind their masks, they all speak of Russia.

7

An Extraordinary Creative Partnership: Stravinsky and Balanchine

December 1924, Paris. In a large salon at Misia Sert's apartment.
A small group of principal dancers has recently arrived in Berlin
from the Mariinsky Theatre, welcomed by the many White Russian
refugees there. They are on a three-month tour showcasing their
work. But they have no intention of returning to the Soviet Union
once their duties are over. Life in the West is too good. News of the
talented troop has reached Diaghilev in Paris, who dispatches his
secretary Boris Kochno to check them out. At a performance in
London Kochno's eye is caught by a twenty-year-old Russian-
Georgian dancer and choreographer named Georgi Balanchivadze.
Excitedly he relays his findings back to Diaghilev. And so, at the
end of the year, the young Soviets find themselves auditioning for
Diaghilev and Serge Lifar in Paris. Balanchivadze dances his own
choreography to the music of Skryabin. Lifar is smitten. 'We must
take these youngsters!' he cries, and Diaghilev agrees to recruit
them on the spot. He, too, has noticed the twenty-year-old, from
whom he is eager to hear news of the motherland. He wants him
to be the company's ballet master. 'Now he is in the West, I shall
call him George Balanchine', Diaghilev thinks to himself.[1]

May 1925. Monte Carlo. Rehearsal studio of the Ballets Russes.
'Would you like to do a Stravinsky ballet?' Diaghilev asks Balanchine.
The young ballet master does not hesitate in accepting. He has long
known and admired Stravinsky's work. He loves *Pulcinella*. He has
recently been preparing a production of it but had to abandon it

when he left the Soviet Union. He has danced in *The Firebird*. At the age of fourteen in Petrograd he even took a role in *The Nightingale* under the direction of Meyerhold. Diaghilev now wants him to remake *The Song of the Nightingale*, the symphonic poem that Stravinsky created from the music of acts Two and Three of the opera, first staged by Massine with the Ballets Russes in 1920. The decor by Henri Matisse is ready and waiting for the revival. And Stravinsky himself – despite the fact that he has never been entirely persuaded that *The Song* is suited to dancing – is anxious to ensure it is executed precisely according to his wishes. He will, for the first time, be conducting the performances of this work. The company understands only too well how exacting the composer can be. But Balanchine is not daunted.

Stravinsky, now living nearby in Nice and recently returned from a demanding concert tour of America and Europe, regularly drops in on rehearsals. It is in the dance studio that Balanchine and Stravinsky first meet. The composer sits at the piano and begins to play *The Song of the Nightingale*. 'That's the way it should be', he says emphatically, looking up at Balanchine. 'The tempo should be like that.' Balanchine has an excellent musical ear. After all, his father is a composer who, like Stravinsky, studied with Rimsky-Korsakov, and Balanchine has himself only recently graduated as a pianist and composer from the Petrograd Conservatoire. He memorizes everything Stravinsky has played him. Stravinsky leaves, and the rehearsal begins. Balanchine prides himself on being able to make the ballet exactly as the composer wants it. A little later, Diaghilev enters the studio to watch his young ballet master at work. 'No!' he cries, 'This is the wrong tempo!' And he starts to bang his bamboo cane on the floor at a slower speed. 'No, Sergey Pavlovich,' Balanchine insists indignantly, 'that's not true. Stravinsky wanted it faster, so that's how I made it.' This riles Diaghilev. 'Well *I* don't want that!' and he bangs his cane again at his own tempo. Balanchine has little choice. He has to change everything to keep Diaghilev happy. He owes so much to Diaghilev, he needs to remain loyal to him, even though he knows deep down that the great impresario actually understands little about dance. But when Stravinsky arrives at the next rehearsal, he is horrified by what he discovers. 'What's the matter with you?' he shouts at Balanchine. 'I told you this is the wrong tempo.'

It was an inauspicious start. There is little evidence from their first encounter that the Stravinsky–Balanchine partnership would become one of the most enduring and successful artistic collaborations of the twentieth century and would result in some of the most exciting work ever made for the ballet stage. Though in recent years some critics have begun to challenge this accepted view of their shared achievements,[2] and while it is certainly possible to exaggerate the common ground between these two brilliant and strong-willed men, it is also true to say that their agreement on such aesthetic matters as 'classical order', and on the temporal dimension of music and dance resulted in an extraordinary unity of creative vision. Their three great classical ballets – *Apollo*, *Orpheus* and *Agon* – stand as witness. 'If I could write music,' Balanchine once wrote, 'it seems to me this is how I would want it to sound.'[3] This is an uncharacteristically self-effacing observation given that Balanchine did indeed write music very well, but it reveals just how much his own artistic instincts resonated with Stravinsky's. For his part, Stravinsky trusted Balanchine deeply: 'I do not see how one can be a choreographer unless, like Balanchine, one is a musician first.'[4] Stravinsky would listen to Balanchine; they planned projects in detail together; he would even change his music at Balanchine's suggestion, something this all-controlling composer would do for no one else. Many of Stravinsky's most celebrated scores were initiated and guided by this man 22 years his junior.

Both artists had begun as progressive modernists, Stravinsky before the war pre-eminently with *The Rite of Spring*, Balanchine in the early 1920s with work inspired by the experimental choreography

Léon Bakst,
Isadora Duncan Dancing, c. 1908.

of Kasyan Goleizovsky, whose near-nude dancers were placed in abstract formations amid constructivist decor. For both Balanchine and Stravinsky their 'discovery of the past' in the interwar years transformed their thinking and led to a paring down of their musical and choreographic languages. In particular, their shared discovery of classical antiquity put them directly in touch with broader developments in interwar Art Deco Europe.

Many of the artists in Paris in whose circle Stravinsky moved were turning to classical subject-matter in the years of the First World War and after: Apollinaire, Debussy, Cocteau, Gide, Milhaud, Picasso, Satie, to name but a few. Stravinsky would eventually follow their example when he worked with Cocteau on *Oedipus Rex* as a result of having seen his *Antigone*. But this was, of course, by no means Stravinsky's first encounter with classical art. He had for more than a decade been working in the midst of an emerging Paris Art Deco culture that referenced and reinterpreted antiquity. Indeed, the importance of classical models as the basis for a new art, for modernism, had been at the heart of the early productions of the Ballets Russes, most notably in Tcherepnin's *Narcisse* (1911) and Ravel's *Daphnis et Chloé* (1912). Their designer had been Léon Bakst, one of the architects of *Mir iskusstva*, who in 1909 had published in the third edition of the journal *Apollon* an essay entitled 'The Paths of Classicism in Art'.[5] Here he gave a prescient vision of the post-war synthesis of high art and haute couture that would be witnessed in such places as *Antigone*: 'Fashion is everywhere that art is to be found.' In this regard it is fascinating to note that Bakst (along with Diaghilev, Benois and Fokine) had been deeply impressed by Isadora Duncan dancing barefoot, 'in a revealing Greek tunic', in St Petersburg as early as December 1904. 'Duncanism' (a 'violent revolt against Petipa's routine', in Nouvel's words) took a strong hold on the Ballets Russes.[6] Bakst saw the art of the future as being 'deliberately uncomplicated', moving towards 'a new and very simple form'. Artists will 'return, like the Greeks of Periclean Athens, to proclamations of the beauty of nature'. Bakst heralds the birth of 'a new classical art'. Duncan, it should be recalled, along with Nijinsky, was to reappear as a classical goddess above the entrance to the very temple of the new, the Théâtre des Champs-Élysées.

The modernity of Stravinsky's new classical art was celebrated in fashionable quarters. This is caught by a review of *Perséphone* from 1934 in London's *Daily Telegraph*, where Richard Capell writes of Stravinsky as 'the musician par excellence of modern life . . . *Persephone* is trivial but ingenious. Ingenious and trivial, knowing and sceptical, half human and half mechanised – is not modern life all that, like Stravinsky's music?' Others, however, remained perplexed by Stravinsky's apparent turning away from progressive modernism. Leonid Sabaneyev, for example, writing in the *Musical Times* of *Apollo* a year after its premiere, was scathing of Stravinsky's volte-face: 'the Bolshevik, the Lenin and Trotsky of music has become a peaceful *rentier* spending the rest of his days in a suburban villa.' It has to be acknowledged that there is more than just a little of the suburban French Art Deco interior in this elegant, stylish and classical work. But did *Apollo* really signal the disappearance of the revolutionary Stravinsky? For his part, Capell was perceptive in identifying the remnants of the mechanical *Rite* in the neoclassical *Perséphone*, just as Rivière and others had detected the *Rite*'s nascent classicism. In keeping with the general Art Deco spirit, Stravinsky and Balanchine embraced the classical past, not to repeat it but to reinvent it, turning it to their own modern purposes.

Apollon musagète (or more simply *Apollo*, as Diaghilev renamed it) was Stravinsky's first collaboration proper with Balanchine. It was written mainly in Nice during the latter part of 1927 and completed in January 1928. It shares many of the characteristics of its immediate predecessor *Oedipus Rex*, but now in the context of a wordless ballet. It was commissioned by the great American patron of chamber music Elizabeth Sprague Coolidge to be premiered in the auditorium of the Library of Congress in Washington, DC, which she had endowed and which still carries her name. Angered by Stravinsky's disloyalty in composing a ballet for someone other than himself, Diaghilev resorted to rubbishing the composer's new-found supporter.

'This American woman is completely deaf.'
'She may be deaf, but she pays,' Stravinsky snapped back.
'You're always thinking of money,' grumped Diaghilev.

And, of course, Stravinsky was more than happy to accept the commission fee ('only' $1,000), despite the fact that he had little interest in the Washington premiere of 27 April 1928, which he did not attend, as he was conducting *Oedipus Rex* in Europe. Nonetheless, the physical limitations of the venue of the original commission may well have prompted some of the characteristic restrictions of the score, even though the composer's attention had long been focused on the Ballets Russes production to be given in Paris in June that same year. Very early in the work's gestation it would seem that Stravinsky had imagined Lifar dancing the role of Apollo, and he later generously acknowledged that the success of the ballet was attributable both to his dancing and also to the beautiful choreography of Balanchine. For Balanchine, *Apollon musagète* marked a creative epiphany that enabled him to pare down his modernist choreographic style.

> *Apollon* I look back on as the turning point of my life. In its discipline and restraint, in its sustained oneness of tone and feeling the score was a revelation. It seemed to tell me that I could dare not to use everything, that I, too, could eliminate.[7]

Stravinsky had decided 'to compose a ballet founded on moments or episodes in Greek mythology plastically interpreted by dancing of the so-called classical school'. Following the 'Prologue' depicting the Birth of Apollo, the three Muses Calliope, Polyhymnia and Terpsichore are introduced, before the work proceeds through a series of conventional variations entirely in keeping with the traditions of the classical ballet. A 'Coda' is reached for all four dancers before the final 'Apotheosis' in which, simply, Apollo leads the three muses towards Parnassus. There is thus a stripping away of any meaningful narrative. What is left is a kind of abstract meditation on classical themes, figures and dances. (One might almost be tempted to rename it *Apollon et sa méditation*, recalling Bourdelle's bas-relief at the Théâtre des Champs-Élysées.) Such a description is equally appropriate to Balanchine's restrained, sculptural choreography, where music and dance are unified in the expression of pure, classical beauty. Stravinsky himself designated *Apollo* a *ballet blanc*, a term derived from the most classical form of nineteenth-century ballet and applied to scenes in which the female dancers are dressed all in white; here he uses it to refer to a music that eschews contrast, pares down the scoring to just strings and employs principally diatonic ('white-note') harmony.

And how did Stravinsky achieve this sense of order as symbolized by the Greek god Apollo? By making it his most thoroughly French work to date. He explicitly turned his back on his own earlier music by trying, as he later said, 'to discover a melodism free of folk-lore'. One means of achieving this was to look to French poetry: the 'real subject' of *Apollo*, he claimed, is 'versification'. Each dance explores a basic iambic (short–long) pattern; the 'Variation of Calliope' is headed by two lines from Nicolas Boileau, poet at the court of Louis XIV, and takes the twelve-syllable lines of the alexandrine as its rhythmic model. It also references French Baroque dances, such as the ouverture style of the opening 'Birth of Apollo' or the pavane-like second 'Variation of Apollo'. But ultimately this speaks of the present, not of the past. This white-note Hellenism points more to Satie than Lully: as Paul Griffiths quips, the 'Gallic spirit of *Apollo* is a complex superimposition of Lully and Delibes, *Daphnis* and the Ritz'.[8] Stravinsky and Balanchine had turned a Greek god into French chic.

Or at least, that is what sits on the surface. But the final 'Apotheosis' opens a window onto something beyond the merely playful and decorative. At one level, an apotheosis at the end of a classical ballet is to be expected, and there are certainly echoes here of Tchaikovsky's *Sleeping Beauty*. In keeping with *Apollo*'s

Apollo (danced by Serge Lifar) with the three muses in Balanchine's choreography of *Apollon musagète*, June 1928.

scenario, the notion of apotheosis suggests the process of transformation into a god, the release from the earthly towards the divine. This is signalled by the heroic key of D major and the Baroque fanfare-character of what Eric Walter White has dubbed the 'Olympian theme'. The music early on is quite clearly hymnal. And yet, below these conventional signs of triumph and closure, the music pulls in a different direction. D major is less certain than it might at first seem, as triads of G major and B minor also circulate freely and simultaneously. The music cannot easily move forward. And, in unexpectedly expressive appoggiaturas, a personal voice begins to emerge from behind the Baroque mask. All this makes the appearance of the Olympian theme less triumphal than might first have been supposed. It takes on a regretful character, as if it is not what it should be, as if something has been lost. Over an unchanging D-pedal, it is a hollow gesture of triumph, soft, at a distance.

Towards the end of the 'Apotheosis' a four-note dotted figure is fractured from the Olympian theme – like a shard from Lully perhaps, a frozen motif – and starts to repeat obsessively, suggesting a lament. It is just one of an entirely new, layered texture of repeating figures, all moving at their own speeds, that simply keep turning in a mechanical way. The D major of apotheosis is side-stepped. The music ends on a triad of B minor, but it resolves little, since the conflicting triads of D major and G major remain implicitly in play. Is this Capell's 'knowing and sceptical, half human and half mechanised'? Whereas the mechanical in the 'Sacrificial Dance' had been dehumanizing, here the mechanical repetitions suggest something melancholic, distant, lost. The music is not violently ripped apart as at the end of *The Rite of Spring* but slowly attenuates and fades. In the wake of the First World War, another *Rite of Spring* would not have been possible – one might say that the destructive consequences of the *Rite* had been all too quickly and tragically realized. Even the hope of apotheosis was now in vain. The Baroque – so strongly present for most of the work – now fragments; time itself seems to come to a halt. The standing on a B-minor triad might appear to give temporary consolation, but the memory of what has been lost is not wiped away. B minor seems, rather, to point to an absence, not a presence. It seems to sing of exile.

In 1946, following another terrible war, Stravinsky and Balanchine, now both resident in the USA, turned to Apollo's son

Orpheus. It is the lamenting Orpheus who is encountered at the start of the ballet named after him, almost as if picking up the melancholic mood left suspended two decades earlier at the end of *Apollo*. 'Orpheus weeps for Eurydice. He stands motionless, with his back to the audience.' We hear his lyre, represented by the sounds of the harp, playing repeated falling lines in a conventional sign of lament. It echoes outward into the strings, who linger over the notes of the harp.

The deaths of the youthful Orpheus and Eurydice took on particular resonance in the violent twentieth century. Many artists had turned to myth as a way of coming to terms with events that were, literally, unspeakable. In the years during and following the First World War, Cocteau, the painter Oskar Kokoschka and the poet Rainer Maria Rilke, to name just three of many, all gave their own voices to Orpheus' laments. In 1925 Cocteau had completed his tragicomic play *Orphée*, which was, as already noted, the catalyst for Stravinsky's first work on a classical, mythical subject. In the late 1940s, at much the same time that Stravinsky was contemplating Orpheus, Cocteau returned to *Orphée*, reworking it as a much darker film, in which Orpheus is a celebrated yet despised poet in post-Second World War Paris. Vivid reminders of the Nazi Occupation are everywhere: in the black-clad, motorcycling messengers of death; in the stone-throwing mob of Bacchantes; in the tribunal of the Judges of the Dead; and in the menacing music of Georges Auric. Painful memories of recent events are mediated through the ancient story.

It is telling that Stravinsky began work on his *Orpheus* within a year of the end of the Second World War. Though the idea for the subject came from Balanchine, it struck a chord with Stravinsky at that particular moment. Never one to reveal his true feelings, he found that the mask of Orpheus enabled him to come to terms with both a series of tragic personal losses and his anxieties for the world situation during the war years. He would still surely have felt the tragedy of the late 1930s, when in rapid succession his first daughter, first wife and mother had all died. An émigré for a second time, Stravinsky experienced the horrors and privations of war only at a distance. Separated from his family in Europe, with both his sons now signed up to the French army, he followed from afar the terrifying and destructive siege of his native city of Leningrad. And it is a sense of distance, too, that in general characterizes the apparently timeless *Orpheus*. Yet, beneath this universalized ritual, the work seems to speak more personally and of its time. It is striking that, as Craft was the first to observe, *Orpheus* is Stravinsky's first score after *The Firebird* in which the term *espressivo* occurs frequently.

The origins of *Orpheus* in fact go back at least a decade, to when Balanchine and the writer and impresario Lincoln Kirstein (who had been instrumental in bringing Balanchine to America as a result of having seen the Ballets Russes production of *Apollo*) first begged Stravinsky to write a sequel to *Apollo*. It was Kirstein who eventually commissioned the work for the newly founded Ballet Society, precursor to the New York City Ballet. In April 1946 Balanchine and Stravinsky worked side-by-side on the scenario and timings. Music and choreography emerged simultaneously. They developed a scenario that starts with Orpheus weeping at Eurydice's funeral and ends with another apotheosis where Apollo appears, 'wrests the lyre from Orpheus and raises his song heavenwards'. The music throughout is restrained, distanced. The sense of formality is reinforced by, for example, the hymn-like frame provided by prologue and epilogue, and the importance throughout of the craft of counterpoint. The designer eventually chosen for the premiere production was the Japanese-American Isamu Noguchi, a sculptor whose abstract geometric sets, costumes and masks perfectly matched the distilled, ritualistic purity of Stravinsky's music and Balanchine's dances.

The only really violent music in the work is the second 'Pas d'action', where the 'Bacchantes attack Orpheus, seize him and tear him to pieces'. But even here the music is disciplined. *Orpheus* offers not the depiction of the violence of war, but rather reflections on war and death. The violent, mechanical repetitions, ostinatos and rhythmic energy of the *Rite* are still to be heard, but now with a sense of detachment. This, above all else, is what Greek myth gave to Stravinsky: not a turning back to ancient Greece, but a universal story retold for a new age. And this myth in particular gave him the context in which he could sing his laments of loss. In the 'Air de danse' Orpheus sings for the loss of Eurydice. To the accompaniment of the lyre, a pair of obbligato oboes give voice to a deeply melancholic lament, weaving lines round each other in grief, echoing a Bach Passion aria. Stravinsky glances back to the eighteenth century, but in so doing he highlights the chasm between his own time and Bach's, thus articulating a mood of uncertainty and alienation entirely in keeping with his modern age.

The final ballet in this Greek trilogy, *Agon* (1953–7), is the last work made by Stravinsky in close collaboration with Balanchine, who commissioned it with Kirstein for the New York City Ballet. (Stravinsky himself resisted the idea that it should be considered part of a trilogy, which was the desire of Balanchine and Kirstein.) Though in many respects quite different from *Apollo* and *Orpheus*, *Agon* nonetheless represents the logical outcome of the paring down of his musical language that had begun in Switzerland during the First World War. The abstraction, the 'classical purity' of the 'white' *Apollo* and the simplicity of *Orpheus* are taken yet further to produce an entirely abstract ballet. There is no plot, no scenario. It is musico-balletic architecture, jointly conceived by its creators. In Balanchine's original production there is not even a set as such; there are no special costumes as the dancers perform in their rehearsal clothes. Stravinsky later likened the choreography to a painting by Mondrian. It is thus an abstract meditation on the idea of dance, and on the idea of Greek myth as contest, game or struggle (the meaning of the title, derived in part from Stravinsky's reading of T. S. Eliot's *Sweeney Agonistes: Fragments of an Aristophanic Melodrama*). Taking as one of its starting points a pair of seventeenth-century French manuals on dance and music by, respectively, François de Lauze and Marin Mersenne, it becomes a dance about dance. *Agon* is also a game of twelves: twelve dancers, twelve dances and elements of Stravinsky's own interpretation of the twelve-note compositional method made famous by Arnold Schoenberg. All this suggests new levels of abstraction, of order, of discipline, of compositional objectification. Apollo, it would seem, had finally taken full control. It is as if, more than a decade and a half on, Stravinsky had now fully realized the aesthetic manifesto set out in the *Poetics of Music*:

> What is important for the lucid ordering of the work – for its crystallization – is that all the Dionysian elements which set the imagination of the artist in motion and make the life-sap rise must be properly subjugated before they intoxicate us, and must finally be made to submit to the law: Apollo demands it.[9]

There is anecdotal evidence to suggest that, in the later 1940s and early 1950s, married to Vera, free for a while of illness and enjoying the warm California weather, Stravinsky was at his happiest. Photographs now caught him smiling. Though still always the outsider, he nonetheless lived longer in the one place than anywhere else in his life: 1260 North Wetherly Drive, Beverly Hills. He and Vera were domestically content in their unprepossessing little house – an American take on a Mediterranean villa – amid a colourful menagerie of a cat, chickens and caged love birds, as if late in life he had come to terms with his émigré status. This is captured to an extent in the exuberant playfulness of *Agon*. Yet there is still something disconcertingly

Igor and Vera Stravinsky with George Balanchine, 1260 North Wetherly Drive, Los Angeles, 1944.

'eccentric, aloof, nostalgic, deliberately untimely' about the work, the very features that George Steiner has claimed distinguish the exile.[10] Just listen to the 'Gailliarde' (the published score retains Stravinsky's misspelling of the French *gaillarde*). Its 'eccentric' inverted texture of low strings sounding high evokes the courtly seventeenth century but in distorted fashion, almost as if the dance has been frozen in an Art Deco frieze. Even the archaic ('deliberately untimely') notation is out of place. And it sits within the eclectic mix of tonal, atonal and serial music of the work as a whole. An 'exile is always out of place', writes Edward Said.[11] Despite having acclimatized to his new existence, *Agon* appears still to point towards Stravinsky's deracinated sense of self. To the extent

Stravinsky outside 1260 North Wetherly Drive, photographed by Vera Stravinsky, 1946.

that, as Said proposes, we 'have become accustomed to thinking of the modern period itself as spiritually orphaned and alienated, the age of anxiety and estrangement', Stravinsky here acts as one of its principal spokesmen. Like the ancient Orpheus, Stravinsky is continually turning back, but in so doing he is only ever confronted with his present losses. Sometimes he laments them; sometimes, as in the 'Gailliarde', he might find momentary solace in the past. Yet, twice exiled, his sense of alienation is hardly lessened.

In Balanchine Stravinsky found more than just the ideal artistic collaborator. He found someone who could present him with ideas that spoke directly to his creative instincts, who could give form to his unspoken creative ambitions. As a musician and a Russian, Balanchine was well positioned to see behind Stravinsky's masks. It is perhaps in these three 'Greek' ballets made with Balanchine that Stravinsky most fully represented the anxieties and losses both of late modernity and of his own twofold emigration. The sense of distance achieved in these works articulates an alienation that often manifests itself as something melancholic, peeping out from behind the masks of order, formalism and objectivity that he wore so frequently in public. This is witnessed most obviously in the subject-matter of *Orpheus*, but even in this work the sense of restraint is very powerful: Orpheus is not expressing loss directly (despite the *espressivos*), but reflecting on it at a distance, in melancholic mode. In all three of these works, Greek antiquity has nothing to do with history; ancient Greece is an idea, a utopian ideal, that stands for an inaccessible past, and associated values of order, wholeness and unity, from which the late modern age has become alienated. Stravinsky's reinvention of Greek classicism carries a double bind. First, it recognizes that that unified past has been lost forever, even while expressing the desire (the need, even) for the restoration of its values of order. It is a desire, however, that is destined to fail, as heard in the apotheoses at the end of both *Apollo* and *Orpheus*. The same could be argued for Stravinsky's re-invention of all manner of music from the past. The seductive surfaces of his neoclassical works might initially suggest a regression. But in ways that echo the Art Deco milieu in which he moved, it is the dialogue between past and present that is crucial, the fragile, even tragic confrontation of new and old values. This forms a highly pertinent expression both of modernist aesthetics and of the post-war world. And it was through his unique working partnership with Balanchine – their shared values and mutual understanding – that he was able to realize this. Secondly, and more personally, as an émigré as much of his own making as victim of political circumstance, Stravinsky appropriated these exemplars of high Western European culture in order to distance himself from his own native 'backwaters'; yet the myths (like the music) he came to inhabit were not his own, and he remained distanced from those too. Home, for Stravinsky, was no longer defined geographically, if it ever had been; it had become a state of mind.

8

Another War, Another Country

A dark cloud hung over Paris during the summer of 1938. Germany had annexed Austria and was pressing her claim on the Sudetenland. Anxiously, France began to mobilize a million of her reservist troops. Only twenty years after the end of the last terrible conflagration, war in Europe was once again on the horizon.

As Stravinsky had discovered in 1914, war – or even the threat of it – had dire consequences for creative and performing artists, reliant as they were on concert work and commissions to make a living. Opportunities were drying up rapidly in Europe. His one bright hope was America, where he had representatives working on his behalf, but few concrete offers were yet materializing. The USA was by now quite familiar to Stravinsky, and many of his close friends and associates had settled there. Stravinsky had already made three successful American concert tours. The first had taken place in early 1925, when he appeared as pianist and conductor in six East Coast and Midwest cities. During that trip he also signed his first ever recording contract, with the Brunswick record company. Like his work in the 1920s 'recording' his music on pianola rolls for, successively, the Pleyel and Aeolian companies, his recording activities as composer-conductor over the ensuing decades would prove to be a lucrative means of supporting himself as well as extending the reach of his music to new audiences. On his second visit to the USA in 1935 Stravinsky traversed the entire country from New York to Los Angeles, from Minneapolis to Fort

Worth, accompanying the violinist Samuel Dushkin and conducting. Two years after that he returned, again with Dushkin, to undertake a similar tour, beginning in Canada and ending by conducting the premiere of his 'ballet in three deals', *Jeu de cartes*, at the Metropolitan Opera in New York. There had also been a regular flow of commissions from the USA, most recently the Concerto in E-flat 'Dumbarton Oaks', and he was hopeful of securing an American commission for the symphony he had been sketching since 1937. Now, thanks to the advocacy of his devoted champion and former colleague from the École Normale Nadia Boulanger, he had been invited to take up the Charles Eliot Norton Professorship of Poetry at Harvard University in the 1939–40 academic year. This was a prestigious and lucrative visiting position whose previous occupants had included such prominent figures as T. S. Eliot and Robert Frost. Established in 1925, the primary responsibility of the occupant of the Norton Chair was to deliver six lectures on 'poetry in the broadest sense'.

But another dark cloud was hanging over Stravinsky's life. Catherine's illness had become progressively more serious and painful, and necessitated ever lengthier stays at the sanatorium in Sancellemoz in the Haute Savoie, keeping her in lonely isolation from her family in Paris. Their daughter Lyudmila, who had given them their first grandchild, Catherine (Kitty), in early 1937, was also suffering with tuberculosis; when she contracted pleurisy, she too was dispatched to a sanatorium not far from Sancellemoz. Stravinsky himself had been warned to keep a serious watch on the condition of his lungs. Both Catherine and Lyudmila eventually returned to the Paris apartment, but were too ill to run the household, so Stravinsky's mother took charge of affairs, despite the fact that her health was also failing. Lyudmila died at the apartment on 30 November 1938 at the age of just 29 while Stravinsky and Soulima were away in Rome giving a concert. The loss had a devastating impact on Catherine, who grew ever weaker over the following months, and she too passed away, on 2 March 1939, surrounded by Stravinsky, his surviving children and his mother. Stravinsky was a broken man, according to Denise (despite the fact that less than 24 hours earlier, with Catherine's passing imminent, he had slipped out of the apartment to spend time with Vera). Catherine's death marked the end of Stravinsky family life at the rue du Faubourg Saint-Honoré. Anna moved out with Soulima and Madubo, and on 7 June 1939, at the age of 84, she died, while Stravinsky and Milène were now also being treated at the Sancellemoz sanatorium. The outbreak of war just a few months later ensured, in Denise's words, that the protagonists of the Stravinsky family saga would be scattered to the four winds.

Stravinsky later declared, with good reason, that this was the most tragic period of his life. Despite all the upheavals, ill health and bereavements, however, he continued to work. The first movement of his symphony was completed just a month after his wife's death, the second (slow) movement after his mother's death, though there was still no prospect of a premiere. His work, it would seem, played a therapeutic role: without it, he claimed, he would not have survived these difficult days, though he was also quick to stress that the symphony should not be considered an 'exploitation' of his grief. Throughout this time he was still at Sancellemoz. He received family visits. Vera arrived in July, much to the disgust of Stravinsky's children, who considered it inappropriate soon after their mother's death. And he was working on his Norton lectures. He had commissioned Souvtchinsky to draft them, and then called on the help of the composer and critic Roland-Manuel, who was summoned to Sancellemoz to work with Stravinsky on the French version. Later revised and published as *Poétique musicale* (*Poetics of Music* in English translation), the text was ghosted entirely by Roland-Manuel but carries the traces of the thinking both of Stravinsky himself (his unmistakable comments on performers and conductors) and of Souvtchinsky (notably an important discussion of musical time derived from the philosophy of Henri Bergson). With their work complete, and with Stravinsky finally discharged from the sanatorium, he and Vera headed back to Paris at the start of September, just as France and Britain declared war on Nazi Germany.

Paris was again in a state of high anxiety. After the tranquillity of the Rhone Alps, the noise and hardships of a wartime city were too much for Stravinsky. Air-raid sirens sounded in the middle of the night, necessitating hasty descents to the cellar. Fresh food was already in short supply. So he and Vera took refuge in Nadia Boulanger's house at Gargenville while preparations were made for his journey to America to deliver his lectures. With German U-boats now active in the North Atlantic, he was not even sure he would get there. Nevertheless he set sail from Bordeaux on 25 September aboard the *Manhattan*, arriving in New York five days later. Vera was left behind and would join him as soon as her papers were in order. Unbeknown to him at the time, this marked the beginning of his second emigration. He would not set foot again on European soil for more than a decade.

Having found accommodation in Cambridge, Massachusetts, Stravinsky embarked on his lecturing and teaching at Harvard, as well as concert work in Boston and New York and on the West Coast. Vera finally arrived on 13 January 1940. They were married in a simple civil ceremony in Boston on 9 March, just a year after the death of Stravinsky's first wife, and promptly put in their applications for American citizenship. It would seem that Stravinsky had little intention of using the return portion of his transatlantic liner ticket. On 25 March the *Boston Daily Globe* was reporting that 'in May the Stravinskys will journey to Los Angeles, there to make their home during the remainder of their stay in this country' – a remainder that was, in Vera's case, to last more than four decades.

Stravinsky photographed by Arnold Newman, New York, 1946.

The entry of the Wehrmacht into Paris on 14 June 1940 made the Stravinskys' permanent sojourn in America well-nigh inevitable, despite the fact that they were cut off from family with scant news of their whereabouts. They took up temporary residence in Beverly Hills off Wilshire Boulevard, before moving 4 kilometres north, to the other side of Sunset Boulevard, into a single-storey house at 1260 North Wetherly Drive, which was to become their home for nearly 30 years. It was a whitewashed building accessed via brick steps leading up to a simple front door with large windows opening onto a well-kept garden that was surrounded by a wooden fence. Consciously or otherwise, Stravinsky seemed to have chosen for himself a little piece of California that reminded him of his beloved summer home left behind long ago in Ustilug. In the peace of this modest abode, in a study surrounded by the familiar books, pictures and memorabilia from his life, Stravinsky would compose at his upright piano all his late, great works. It must have seemed the most unlikely place for these cultured, cosmopolitan Europeans, used to servants and the trappings of luxury, to re-graft their roots. After all, unlike so many of the other European émigrés who had also found their way to Los Angeles – Arnold Schoenberg and Thomas Mann among them – the Stravinskys were not genuine refugees by dint of racial or political oppression. They had made a free choice to sever their ties with war-torn Europe and to live in this 'hideous but lively' city. But it suited them well, not least the southern California climate, which gave respite to Stravinsky's poor health and nagging fear of tuberculosis. And perhaps in Hollywood, as the centre of the American entertainment industry and a magnet for the wealthy, Stravinsky secretly hoped he would be able to continue to rub shoulders with the latest celebrities and power brokers, just as he had done in the salons of interwar Paris.

Above all else, Stravinsky needed a secure environment in which to compose, and this was no longer possible in Europe. He had experienced the privations of war once before and did not wish to repeat the experience. He longed for order, as the text of the *Poetics of Music* proclaimed, and he expected his family to understand and tolerate this, even if it meant abandoning them, just as he had expected Catherine to tolerate his relationship with Vera for the sake of his art. Further, his growing success as a performer in America contrasted sharply with the lack of concert-giving opportunities in occupied Europe. This reorientation was compounded by negative reactions to his recent music; American audiences and critics, by contrast, generally greeted his new work with enthusiasm. Ever the opportunist, Stravinsky needed to take advantage of this situation. With his new wife it was time to make a new start in the New World.

In fact, his first work completed in the USA was the symphony conceived on tour there but whose first two movements had already been written in Europe. Sponsorship had finally been forthcoming to enable a performance. The premiere of the Symphony in C, as it was to be known, would be given to mark the fiftieth anniversary of the founding of the Chicago Symphony Orchestra, and so Stravinsky set to work composing the final two movements. The symphony is therefore a work of transition, straddling the move from Europe to America. Some commentators believe that this is somehow recorded in the music, noting a distinct change in style. The vivacious scherzo is certainly less obviously 'classical' than the opening movements. Stephen Walsh goes so far as to suggest that the third and fourth movements 'evoke fleetingly the scurry and glitter of celluloid America'[1] – if true, a remarkably instant act of assimilation on Stravinsky's part, but at least in keeping with his later claim that certain passages might not have occurred to him before he had known the 'neon glitter of Los Angeles's boulevards from a speeding automobile' (first experienced in fact in 1935). The title gives nothing away. Indeed, as his first non-texted, non-programmatic piece for standard orchestra without soloists since his 'test-piece' symphony of 1907, it might be construed as his attempt at last to align himself with the central European symphonic tradition he had just left behind. In outward appearance it is just that: the standard four movements articulate the most basic tonality of C major in keeping with the symphonic works of Haydn, Beethoven and Tchaikovsky it was rumoured he had on his desk. What better models of classical order could one imagine? Nicolas Nabokov recalled an irritable Stravinsky wanting to leave Europe for America, 'where life was still orderly'. At a time of great disruption and personal tragedy, he chose to wear the mask of the 'neutral' symphony. The text of the *Poetics*, written simultaneously with the symphony, corroborates this: it speaks of the composer's concern for the 'rules of the craft', of a 'taste for order and discipline'. The Symphony in C, one might say, delivered this.

The first movement bears all the hallmarks of the classical symphony, more specifically of Beethoven's and Tchaikovsky's first symphonies (both also in C). Its sonata form, its taut thematic and motivic argument, and its key organization display a cohesion in keeping with the Classical-Romantic genre. A Chicago Symphony subscriber, hearing the piece when it was new, could easily have found the title's promise fulfilled, in a work just like Beethoven but with a witty *modernsky* flavour. Behind the mask, however, is something much more ambiguous that is neither symphonic nor in C. The ordered, directed surface gives way to a disconnected sub-structure, where fragments repeat, get stuck in a static present, are trapped anxiously between a classical past that has been lost and an uncertain future. The reiterated Es and Gs that accompany the main theme resist C major (the crucial note C is conspicuous by its absence). The yearning for resolution of the leading note in the main theme is compromised. The leading note represents a longing for what cannot be. An arrival is finally achieved eleven bars before the end of the movement, but a definite sense of closure is contradicted by the final alternating chords, in which the leading note remains simultaneously resolved and unresolved. This lends the music a melancholy air. The first movement's opening motto returns in the final movement as a memory, where it forms the melody to the concluding chorale, itself a familiar (and decidedly un-symphonic) Stravinskian lament. Aside from the final string chord, the chorale is scored for just wind and brass, and could have been lifted straight from the end of the *Symphonies of Wind Instruments*. Far from home, Stravinsky longs nostalgically for Russia. It is a poignant moment. Just as in *Apollo*, the classical past has failed Stravinsky; it refuses to bring him the order he so desires. Like the *Poetics*, the Symphony in C was written in sorrow, in loneliness, in exile. Though it seeks order, it discovers loss.

The hoped-for security in the Land of Opportunity did not arrive quickly. The flow of royalties from Europe had been staunched, and his music had no copyright protection in America. He would soon embark on an extensive project to revise his earlier scores in order to bring them into copyright and start earning him revenues once more. For the present, his personal finances remained on a knife-edge. Once again, he had to adapt. Conducting his own music was one way to bring in money. With the Hollywood studios just round the corner, the commercial route seemed another obvious one to try. *Fantasia* had already been released, and in

October 1940 Stravinsky paid a second visit to Paramount Pictures, where he had first been in 1937, to discuss projects, all of which came to nothing. Hollywood, it would seem, was interested more in Stravinsky's celebrity status than in his music. But in the 1940s he did write a series of pieces based on popular forms and for popular groups. He later tried to distance himself from what Craft referred to as these 'so-called jazz' works: 'these were all journeyman jobs, commissions I was forced to accept because the war in Europe had so drastically reduced the income from my compositions'. But can they be so easily dismissed? There was the Tango for Benny Goodman, the Circus Polka 'For a Young Elephant' at the Barnum & Bailey Circus, *Scènes de ballet* for a Broadway revue, the *Scherzo à la russe* for Paul Whiteman's Band and the 'Ebony' Concerto, again for Benny Goodman. Just as with his ragtime works written during the First World War, it could be argued that these pieces were the product of someone who did not really 'know' American jazz; he found in jazz those aspects of himself he was able to recognize and treated it like any other borrowed musical style. He was learning to speak English in order to assimilate himself into Los Angeles society; in his music he was attempting to 'speak jazz' in order to assimilate himself into American musical culture. What emerged was, as always, Stravinsky. And he found that his 'journeyman' work seeped into his 'art' work too.

'My *Symphony in Three Movements* celebrated my arrival in the United States of America.' By way of recognition of this fact, it incorporates elements of American popular music, most famously the final chord, a Hollywood added-sixth chord if ever there was one. 'Rather too commercial', was his later verdict, goaded on by Craft. Sections of the first and last movements also exploit the rumba, a dance of African-Cuban origin made popular in the U.S. in the 1930s with its characteristic 3–3–2 beat rhythmic pattern. These passages have an exhilarating rhythmic vitality, even though their harmony remains entirely static. In fact, the music here is gloriously octatonic, not an unfamiliar situation in jazz, where this mode is known as the 'diminished scale', but Stravinsky of course knew it from Rimsky. The 'rumba' passage in the first movement alternates chords of E-flat7 and C7, over and over, distantly recalling the Coronation Scene from Musorgsky's *Boris Godunov*. In celebrating America, the émigré looked back once again to Russia.

The Symphony in Three Movements was Stravinsky's first large-scale composition written entirely on American soil. Though often paired with the Symphony in C, it could not be more different. Whereas the Symphony in C aimed, in principle at least, for a unified musical surface, the Symphony in Three Movements is much more eclectic in its musical materials, resulting in a discontinuous, anti-symphonic structure built from sharply contrasting blocks. Cinematic might be an appropriate description for this work written in Hollywood – and, indeed, Stravinsky later claimed that some of its music had been recycled from an aborted film project. The evidence for this is unconvincing, as is his attempt (swiftly contradicted) to impose some sort of war narrative onto the work. Stravinsky's music is always of its time, but never in such a crass, representational way. In any case, the lyrical second movement is a much more straightforward 'classic' neoclassicism, familiar from the French years, and anticipating the kind of writing more extensively employed in his opera *The Rake's Progress*, on which he was to commence work just after the war. Begun in 1942, the Symphony in Three Movements was set aside twice and not finished until August 1945, just as the u.s. was dropping its devastating atomic bombs on Japan and bringing the Second World War to an end. On 28 December 1945 Stravinsky was granted u.s. citizenship. A month later, in his first public appearance as an American, he conducted the premiere of his 'American' symphony with the New York Philharmonic Orchestra, in the very city in which he had landed to begin his second exile.

9

An Opera About Opera

The Rake's Progress is Stravinsky's only full-length piece for the
theatre, and his first major work in the English language. It is
often regarded as his ultimate neoclassical statement, though
Stravinsky himself would have been sceptical of such a description.
"'Neoclassicism?' he once scoffed. "A label that means nothing
whatever. I will show you where you should put it" – and he
gave his derriere a firm pat.'[1] Yet, as so often with Stravinsky's
utterances, this was a defensive outburst and masked a deeper
sensitivity. Stravinsky was aware of the scathing attacks being
made on his neoclassical music by the young Turks of the post-war
European avant-garde. On returning to California from Europe
after the first performances of the *Rake*, he was to experience
a serious crisis of confidence, and would confess to Robert Craft
that he regarded the opera as some kind of an ending. In fact,
both the work's length and its summative nature may well have
come about because Stravinsky at last had uninterrupted time
to devote to an extended composition, for in January 1947 he
had signed a five-year exclusive contract with the publisher Boosey
& Hawkes. This gave him finally the security of a guaranteed
annual income he had so long craved. In this moment Stravinsky
resolved to write an opera in English to consolidate his arrival in
the New World. But it was a task that would give him more trouble
than almost any other composition. It would take him nigh-on
four years to complete, by which time he would be exhausted by

his efforts. While *The Rake's Progress* does indeed represent an ending of a sort for Stravinsky, reflecting on his entire neoclassical output, with hindsight it is also possible to see it as a beginning again, a looking forward to aspects of the more rarefied work of his later years.

While passing through Chicago in May 1947, Stravinsky had come across an exhibition at the Art Institute of prints by William Hogarth, which sparked an idea for a sequence of operatic scenes. Hogarth's original 'novel in paint' of 1735, *The Rake's Progress*, was part of a larger project, Modern Moral Subjects. Like the plays of the time, these series had 'fully worked-out plots, dramatic confrontation and changes of scene, serious and tragic elements juxtaposed, and a high degree of topicality'.[2] They were also, in keeping with the spirit of their age, deeply satirical. Stravinsky instantly recognized their operatic potential. The depiction of the ironic progress of the spendthrift heir of a miser from wealth via debt to madness and death is, in essence, retained in the opera. But it was the melancholic final scene in Bedlam, depicting the last moments of the Rake, that particularly caught Stravinsky's imagination: 'the hero's end in an asylum scratching a fiddle would make a meritorious conclusion to his stormy life.' Ultimately this did not quite find its way into the opera, but it gave Stravinsky the impetus he needed. Hogarth's violinist had struck a chord with him, resonating back at least as far as *The Soldier's Tale*.

The English writer Aldous Huxley, who kept a modest house in Beverly Hills close to that of the Stravinskys, had become a friend and confidant. He and his Belgian wife, Maria, were frequent visitors to North Wetherly Drive. According to Craft, the two men were decidedly unalike. Craft paints a portrait of this seeming giant of a man in the Lilliputian confines of the Stravinsky residence. He also suggests that the 'sovereignty of scientific rationalism, the blueprint of his [Huxley's] intellectual heredity, is a planet away from I.S.'s mystagogic view of human existence'.[3] And yet Huxley's move from Europe to California had prompted an (admittedly quasi-scientific) exploration of mystical experience, as he was to document later in *The Doors of Perception* (1954). This account of the effects of a hallucinogenic drug charts a shift from the 'purely aesthetic, Cubist's-eye view' of his immediate environment towards a 'sacramental vision of reality'.[4] He might almost have written in the same terms of the later neoclassical music of Stravinsky, whose objectivist take on his (musical) environment was nonetheless shaped and coloured by his renewed devotion to the mystical traditions of the Orthodox Church. There was, then, fertile common ground between them. For Stravinsky, always drawn to a fellow émigré, the francophone Huxleys provided a welcome interface between Europe and America; Huxley was to prove instrumental in advising Stravinsky on questions of English language and literature. And when Stravinsky was casting around for a librettist for his English verse opera, it was Huxley who came up with the inspired suggestion of W. H. Auden, another tall English writer, resident in New York and who, like Stravinsky, had acquired U.S. citizenship just the previous year.

Ralph Hawkes, managing director of the New York office of the Boosey & Hawkes publishing house, brokered the deal between the two men, and on 6 October 1947 Stravinsky contacted Auden for the first time, inviting him to prepare a general outline and 'free verse preliminary' for characters and chorus. The restrictions within which he expected Auden to work are spelled out even in their first communication. It was to be a number work, he insisted, not a musical drama. (He obviously wanted to avoid the to-ing and fro-ing that had marred the early stages of commissioning the text for *Oedipus Rex* from Cocteau.) 'Of course there is a sort of limitation as to form in view of Hogarth's style and period. Yet make it as contemporary as I treated Pergolesi in my *Pulcinella*.' Auden was clearly sympathetic to the task. They quickly agreed, however, that the crafting of an opera scenario required more than an exchange of letters, and so on 11 November Auden arrived for a short stay in Hollywood to thrash out the details. Stravinsky recalls with affection the arrival, late at night, of 'this big, blond, intellectual bloodhound', who had of necessity to sleep with his body on the couch and his feet on a chair. They set to work on the scenario next morning fuelled only by cigarettes, coffee and whisky, and the outline was complete in little over a week. The first drafts of each act were to follow in quick

W. H. Auden, Fire Island, New York, 1946.

instalments in January and February, Auden having also enlisted the services of a 'collaborator', as he described Chester Kallman in a letter, 'an old friend of mine in whose talents I have the greatest confidence'. One wonders why Auden felt the need to be quite so coy. Kallman had become his lover in 1939, and they remained companions to the end of Auden's life. It was through the opera lover Kallman that Auden had greatly expanded his knowledge and experience of the genre. Kalmann's influence on the shape of the *Rake* was to be crucial to its ultimate success, and the final text reveals traces of the hands of both writers. Auden principally wrote Rakewell's lines, while Kallman contributed Anne's. As a consequence, John Fuller argues, the opera mirrors their life together, 'reversing their own emotional relationship, which the opera indirectly represents'.[5] Whether Stravinsky ever suspected this remains a matter of conjecture.

Auden and Stravinsky were well matched. In many ways their lives had followed similar paths. Both had arrived in America in 1939. Both had left war-torn Europe of their own volition. Both had forged their reputations as experimental modernists, but then turned towards a more formal, stylized art. In Auden's case this has even been proposed as the beginnings of a postmodernism in his work. And it is true that what 'fascinated and delighted' Stravinsky most about Auden was his sense of play. Stravinsky later observed that, for Auden, the making of poetry was a game: 'All his conversation about Art was, so to speak, *sub specie ludi*.'[6] While this turn of phrase is most likely to be Craft's, the sentiment is nonetheless Stravinsky's. His neoclassical works were governed principally by ideas of ordered, rule-based play or ritual, and so concerned themselves with the formal and symbolic. This helps explain Stravinsky's ongoing identification with pre-Romantic music and culture. Johan Huizinga, in his groundbreaking interwar study of the play-element, argues that such playfulness was at its fullest in the eighteenth century, embodied in men's dress and specifically the periwig, 'one of the most remarkable instances of the play-factor in culture'.[7] Stravinsky, always playful in the way he dressed, adopting the most up-to-date fashions, always changing his mask, was in tune with those times. All the more reason, then, for him to turn to the playful Auden, the master technician and lover of word games, to help bring Hogarth's pictures to life. In Hogarth's *Rake*, the playing of music and games is central; even the marriage is a game of convenience, a charade, an *acte gratuit*. In Auden's *Rake*, 'good or bad, all men are mad; all they say or do is theatre.' Life is a game. To Auden and Stravinsky, a pair of twentieth-century game-players, it offered resonant subject-matter.

The working relationship between Stravinsky and Auden was an unusually happy one. This was in large part a consequence of Auden's recognition of his subordinate role in the process. The librettist's job, he wrote in his first letter to Stravinsky, was 'to satisfy the composer, not the other way round'. More than a decade later, Auden continued to muse that the libretto is 'a private letter to the composer . . . as expendable as infantry to a Chinese general'.[8] When Stravinsky asked for changes or additions that would better suit his musical purposes, Auden willingly obliged. Privately, however, Auden had expressed misgivings about Stravinsky's proposed plot; the final shape and content of the opera betray the strong guiding hand of Auden. Stravinsky's two acts have become three; spoken dialogue has become recitative; Stravinsky's 'choreographic divertissement' at the end of his first act has been transformed into Auden's 'choric parabasis' (in the guise of Mozartian epilogue) at the very end of the work. It is Auden who, with a knowing nod towards Restoration comedy, fashions the hero, girl and villain of the scenario into Tom Rakewell, Anne Trulove and Nick Shadow. And it is Auden who grafts onto Hogarth's quest narrative aspects of, among other sources, classical pastoral (Venus and Adonis), Christian legend (Faust), fairy tale (Mother Goose, the three wishes), circus (a bearded lady), the Bible (the

Devil tempts Jesus to turn stones into bread) and, with the help of Kallman, opera in many different manifestations. Clever it certainly is; whether or not this eclectic mix of sources hangs together, and whether or not Stravinsky was entirely alert to the subtleties of these many allusions, are other questions.

During Auden's first visit *chez* Stravinsky they took time out from their labours to attend an amateur two-piano performance of Mozart's *Così fan tutte* – not then a repertoire work. Much has subsequently been made of the Mozartian references in *The Rake's Progress*, encouraged by Stravinsky's own comments on the matter, and not least by his assertion that 'the *Rake* is deeply involved in *Così*.' There is no doubt that Mozart was much on his mind at the earliest stages, and following Auden's visit he asked his publisher to send the 1930s recordings of Fritz Busch conducting the Da Ponte operas at Glyndebourne, as well as a score of *The Magic Flute*. He also called for scores of Handel's *Messiah* and *Israel in Egypt* and, later, *The Beggar's Opera*. Unsurprisingly, then, the spectre of Mozart stalks the completed *Rake*. The opening pastoral trio, 'The woods are green', begins like much of Mozart's outdoor music and is peppered with Mozartian melodic and harmonic gestures. Fiordiligi and Dorabella's first duet in *Così*, 'Ah guarda, sorella', might well be lurking just below the surface. The graveyard scene in Act Three engages with the encounters between Don Giovanni and the statue of the Commendatore, while the Epilogue references overtly the closing ensemble of *Don Giovanni*.

All this might lead one to suppose that *The Rake's Progress* is little more than *modernsky* Mozart for the bourgeoisie, who like to be challenged, but not too much. Or, at least, bourgeois audiences the world over have continued to clamour for performances of the *Rake* in part because they have convinced themselves that they *are* listening to Mozart with a few wrong notes. And in truth there is little to suggest otherwise in, say, the first banal recitative ('Anne, my dear. – Yes, Father. – Your advice is needed in the kitchen.')

with its conventional *parlando* declamation and first-inversion chords on the harpsichord. If such music were expected to be taken at face value, then Stravinsky deserved every criticism the Boulez circle could hurl at him.

But, as with Hogarth, nothing in Stravinsky is necessarily as it seems. He had frequently demonstrated, most recently in the Symphony in C, that appearances can be deceptive. And so in the *Rake*. Stravinsky is not imitating but dissecting Mozart. The opening Trio sets the tone. That four-note falling figure, those Alberti-style accompaniments, are Mozart dislocated. Complete root-position tonic triads are conspicuous by their absence. Mozart would never, could never have done this. There is a mismatch between the way the instrumental music behaves and the apparently sincere, expressive lines of the singers. 'Love tells no lies.' But the music speaks otherwise: it is as if quotation marks have been placed around the singers' words. Nothing is to be believed. And while the following (literally) kitchen-sink recitative might just be construed as pastiche, the context offered by the work as a whole leads the listener retrospectively to question its sincerity too. This prompts us to return to Stravinsky's comment that 'the *Rake* is deeply involved in *Così*.' Irony is at the heart of *Così*, which plays terrifying games with our sense of what is true and what is illusory. Taken out of context (as it so often is), Mozart's trio 'Soave sia il vento' comes across as one of the most poignant numbers in all opera, as the two sisters wish their lovers a safe sea passage. Don Alfonso joins in without any audible sense of irony. Yet the situation is a deception, engineered by the Mephistophelean Alfonso. How can such beautiful music deceive us? It is entirely sincere and yet it is acting a lie. The music draws us close to the characters but, ironically, we must keep our distance. And so with *The Rake's Progress*. Are we also shown 'flesh and blood' characters in the *Rake*, or do they merely remain the puppets of Auden and Stravinsky? These are not easy questions to answer, and this may be why the experience of watching the *Rake* is a discomfiting, alienating one.

The Rake's Progress as a whole does not present Mozart arranged, pastiched or reinvented, but Mozart alienated. Mozart's 'Age of Gold' cannot be restored, with or without a kiss, as Tom Rakewell would like to think, and as he rather pompously proclaims at the start of the opera. There is an unbridgeable chasm between Mozart's time and Stravinsky and Auden's post-war Age of Uncertainty. Many have commented that the *Rake* seemed an extraordinary work for Stravinsky to have been writing so soon after the Second World War, so apparently disengaged from world events. But, like the recently completed *Orpheus*, far from escaping into ancient Greek mythology or eighteenth-century comedy, the subject-matter and its musical treatment engage allegorically with personal and collective loss, and articulate a melancholic sense of alienation. Orpheus mourns the loss of Eurydice, yearning to be reunited with her, but is nonetheless forced to accept the reality of his alienation. It is striking that at the very end of Tom's life, in his madness, alienated even from himself, believing himself to be Adonis, he invokes Orpheus with appropriately Monteverdian echoes: 'My heart breaks. I feel the chill of death's approaching wing. Orpheus, strike from thy lyre a swan-like music . . .'. Only Anne sticks by him.

Indeed, of all the characters in the *Rake*, it is Anne who appears the most genuine, the only one who remains true to the end. Auden and Kallman may have been more interested in the gay joke of the Bearded Lady than they were in faithful Anne, but not Stravinsky, who provides her with some of the most expressive music of the opera. Who can fail to be moved by her impassioned 'I go to him', ending Act One with a resounding top C? Yet even here, do we not deceive ourselves if we get carried away with the emotion? Is Stravinsky not once again playing with the past? Scene Three begins with woodwind music that is a reworking of the introduction to the work's opening Trio. In itself this is an unexpected gesture, implying a larger-scale musical continuity and dramatic development out of keeping with the opera's avowedly number structure. And this music does not sound like Mozart anymore. The dotted figures are now Russian, not Viennese. This could almost have been lifted from the *Symphonies of Wind Instruments*. The recitative–Aria–'tempo di mezzo'–Cabaletta structure that follows is stock-in-trade nineteenth-century 'Code Rossini' cunningly imitated by Kallman. The music of the Aria ('Quietly night') is a strange hybrid of Bach and Verdi; the Cabaletta ('I go to him') mixes Mozartian melodic poise with the orchestral verve of Donizetti. So what is the listener meant to make of this? Despite the emotive delivery of Anne's lines, the multiple musical allusions pointing in so many different directions seem to undercut their sentiments, distancing the character from us. Even Stravinsky's setting of the text, as so often since his 'rejoicing discovery', works across the natural rhythms of the language, with the effect of highlighting the words *as* words, words as play. Anne's emotions are placed in quotation marks. And it turns out that even the final bel canto top C, set to the word 'heart', was Auden's idea, added by Stravinsky at a late stage to keep his literary collaborators (and, no doubt, his Italian first-night audience) happy. Another game.

So is *The Rake's Progress* just a fable, as the libretto proclaims, a mere pantomime to divert and entertain in the manner of *Renard*? At one level, yes. The characters are cardboard cut-outs – a facet of the work represented virtuosically in David Hockney's Hogarthian sets and costumes for the oft-revived Glyndebourne production of 1975. But there are also significant differences between *Renard* and the *Rake*. *Renard*'s distancing techniques are explicit, in the way they are not in the *Rake*. The opera gets musically darker and more serious as it unfolds, such that one might suppose that Stravinsky *is* allowing the emotion of each character's situation progressively to speak to the listener. The pastiches of the opening become less obvious and more complex the deeper into the work one moves. But the fact that even the most affecting music is undermined in an almost Brechtian manner makes it hard to feel sympathy for any character. Do we care for Anne and Tom? Are we moved by Tom's death? Quite possibly not. Did Stravinsky care for them? That is a more difficult question to answer. The Epilogue, while providing the formal closing frame that Stravinsky so often required, undoes everything that precedes it, as if Stravinsky were saying, 'only joking'. The moral – that the Devil finds work for idle hands – is an empty one, especially in a work written in the shadow of a terrible war. The Epilogue distracts us so that, instead of leaving the auditorium contemplating Tom's fate, we simply hurry to the bar with a smile on our face and a tune in our head.

In July 1948, in the midst of his work on the *Rake*, Stravinsky appeared on the front cover of *Time* magazine, confirming his newfound status as an American celebrity. Echoing his *Autobiography* on the illusion of musical expression, *Time* declared,

David Hockney's design for Glyndebourne of the final 'Bedlam' scene of *The Rake's Progress*, 1975.

> The last thing Stravinsky now wants to do is appeal to the
> senses. He has come to loathe most of the nineteenth century
> romantic composers except Tchaikovsky and Beethoven . . .
> He regards Wagner and his 'heroic hardware' as 'shamelessly
> sensual'.

This was Stravinsky's officially sanctioned persona. And yet here
he is, at this self-same moment, peeping through the cracks in the
many masks he wears in the *Rake*, appealing directly to the senses.
Anne's folk-like lullaby, albeit sung in the guise of Venus, is deeply
touching in its simplicity. Her closing duet with her father ('Every
wearied body must / Late or soon return to dust') transports us
back to a lamenting Russian landscape. Throughout the opera Anne
summons up the pastoral mode in words and music. This pastoral
is neither destructive (*The Rite of Spring*) nor redemptive (Wagner's
'heroic hardware'); rather it suggests a mournful nostalgia for a
lost or imaginary world. Stravinsky the exile identifies with Anne.
And perhaps it is not too farfetched to suggest that Stravinsky also
invests in Anne's simple and undeniably expressive music his
feelings for his own faithful truelove, Vera, just as he had done in
'Sur ce lit' in *Perséphone*.

Finally settled together forever with Vera in America, Stravinsky
was happy, though a happiness tinged, necessarily, with a sense of
loss. The Epilogue places all this at a distance. Perhaps Stravinsky
was just too embarrassed by such a revelation of the senses, reined
in by the *pudeur* regarding all things personal that had governed
his public behaviour throughout his life: he wanted onlookers to
believe that expression, too, was merely another mask. So, at one
level, the *Rake* is just as Baba tells it: theatre about theatre, opera
about opera. But at another level the *Rake* reveals itself as a piece very
much of its time and place. For Auden it is an ironic commentary
on the emptiness of unbridled capitalism, on the futility of freedom
without responsibility. Stravinsky parallels this in so much skilfully

crafted, playful purposelessness. Yet it is more than this, more than just a proto-postmodern game-playing with musical ideas from across the history of opera. It is as though, in the New World, Stravinsky had at last been given licence to take stock of his life. *The Rake's Progress* becomes an allegory of the late-modern world. Two world wars had destroyed any utopian illusion of a civilized society. Only shards of the 'Age of Gold' remain, fragments that can no longer cohere, like the disconnected objects of Rakewell's life in the auction house, shattering the memory of the way things once were. The music makes futile attempts to join things up, most notably in the varied repetitions that reach across Anne's music. But it fails. The melancholic, pastoral landscape of the end of the work acknowledges this. Dislocated, alienated, late-modern man mourns the loss of wholeness, the loss of innocence. 'Modern nostalgia is a mourning for the impossibility of mythical return, for the loss of an enchanted world', observes Svetlana Boym.[9] As in *Orpheus*, revealed here as the tragic complement of the *Rake*, this is surely Stravinsky's lament for a life spent in exile, for the losses of family and homeland? As such, it draws a line under the past for him. But in allowing expression momentarily to voice itself through Anne, Stravinsky is also seeking the possibility of a new future. The comic ending can hardly disguise this. Little wonder, then, that *The Rake's Progress* exhausted Stravinsky.

10

A Crisis and a Way Forward

Mojave Desert, California, 8 March 1952. About 100 kilometres north of Los Angeles. Robert Craft sits behind the wheel. It's Saturday afternoon, and he is driving the Stravinskys home after an outing to Palmdale, where the three of them have taken lunch together in a small restaurant. The Wild West meets Old Europe: cowboy-style spare-ribs have been washed down with a Bordeaux that Stravinsky has brought with him in his Thermos flask. Snow is in the air and, as they drive higher into the San Gabriel mountains that separate the desert from Los Angeles, it begins to settle on the ground too. The conversation takes a sudden chilling turn. Tears are welling up in Stravinsky's eyes; his words catch in his throat. 'I'm afraid I can no longer compose', he declares. '*The Rake's Progress* will be my last work. I don't know what to do.' He realizes he has reached some sort of creative impasse. And he breaks down, and weeps. Vera takes his hand, as she has done on so many previous occasions, and gently reassures him. 'It will pass, Igor', she says, quietly. Whatever his difficulties at this moment, she is sure he will find a way through them.

What prompted Stravinsky's outpouring on this occasion, and precisely what was said, will probably never be known. Vera and Craft were the only witnesses. Stravinsky had never displayed his emotions in this way before, let alone cried. Even Craft's various versions of the story vary on the fact of whether tears were actually shed or not. But what is certain is that this was an important turning point in Stravinsky's life. His fear that he had nothing left to say of originality was a very real one. Much later he reflected on this crisis, which, he said to Craft, was 'brought on by the natural outgrowing of the special incubator in which I wrote *The Rake's Progress* . . . I could not continue in the same strain, could not compose a sequel to *The Rake*, as I would have had to do'.

There was another worry on Stravinsky's mind. It had always mattered to him to be at the forefront of fashion, but he was shocked to discover on his recent long tour of Europe that he was considered 'old hat' by many younger composers. Neoclassicism, which had in the 1920s and '30s been received as modern and chic, was now being represented as a turning away from the progressive values of modernism. Olivier Messaien, a quarter-century younger than Stravinsky, decried neoclassical composers as 'placing around their works a modern sauce that fools the ears of the public, which imagines having heard "modern" music'. Stravinsky's *Apollo* he described as 'like a piece by Lully with a few wrong bass notes'. 'I admire Stravinsky,' he once said, and that was certainly reflected in the analyses of Stravinsky's early works he presented to his classes at the Paris Conservatoire, 'but I believe that *Le Sacre* marked the pinnacle of his genius.'

The composers of the immediate post-war European avant-garde, the majority of whom had studied in *la classe de Messiaen*, regarded Stravinsky as a lost cause, as intolerably retrospective. Stravinsky was, Pierre Boulez later wrote, 'haunted by history'. The young Turks wished to turn their backs on the past, which for them was deeply tainted – certainly for those, like Boulez, who had lived through the Nazi occupation. They proclaimed their avant-garde credentials with a vengeance. Stravinsky's neoclassical music became a particular focus for their ire. In 1945 the angry young men from Messiaen's class organized noisy disruptions of concerts in the Paris Stravinsky Festival, most famously shouting and blowing police whistles during the French premiere of *Four Norwegian*

Moods (composed in 1942). Stravinsky represented that past, not the future.

And there was another player in the crisis, who had just passed over the horizon, of whom Stravinsky was becoming increasingly conscious: Arnold Schoenberg. He was a fellow émigré and a fellow resident of Los Angeles, yet the two never exchanged a word in public or in private during their entire shared time in that city. They had first met in Berlin in 1912, when Stravinsky had expressed his admiration for *Pierrot lunaire*, Schoenberg likewise for *Petrushka*. But across the intervening years hostility had grown between them. Stravinsky once described the serial Schoenberg as 'a chemist of music more than an artistic creator'; for his part, Schoenberg was contemptuous of Stravinsky's brand of neoclassicism. Others sustained the ideological and aesthetic opposition between the two, begun by Lourié in 1926, continued by Theodor Adorno in the 1940s with his influential pair of essays on the two composers published as *Philosophy of New Music*. Yet, for all this, these giants of musical modernism had more in common than either was prepared to admit. Stravinsky was deeply moved by Schoenberg's death in 1951 and, on hearing the news, immediately sent a telegram to Schoenberg's widow expressing his genuine sense of loss. He wanted to attend the funeral, but decided against doing so in case his presence there was misinterpreted as ironic.

For 40 years Stravinsky had dismissed Schoenberg's music as so much Romanticism, so much experiment, so much theory. But there was another reason, aside from the Viennese composer's death, that prompted Stravinsky's renewed interest. Craft was already playing a significant role in promoting and conducting the music of the Second Viennese School in America, music that was little known and rarely performed outside the academy. He had visited Schoenberg in July 1950 at his Brentwood Park home in order to discuss issues of performance. (Stravinsky's name was uttered by neither of them on this occasion.) Schoenberg was

obviously impressed with the young conductor, as well as flattered
by his attention. In his diary Craft records with pride a letter
Schoenberg wrote to the conductor Fritz Stiedry and his wife in
1951: 'My young friend Mr Craft is slowly working himself into my
music by performing my music a lot and finally he will succeed.
I would like to see all my friends encourage such people as Craft.'
In early 1952 Craft conducted a series of Schoenberg memorial
concerts that included the Septet Suite Op. 29 along with Webern's
Quartet Op. 22. Stravinsky attended all the rehearsals. They
obviously made a powerful impression on him, and Craft reports
Stravinsky hinting at a desire to learn more about the Septet
during his Palmdale breakdown. This was the stimulus Stravinsky
had been searching for; this would offer the way out of the crisis.
From this moment on, across the remaining fifteen years of his
creative life, he was to engage with the serial and dodecaphonic
processes he discovered in Schoenberg, in Webern and elsewhere,
and to leave his inimitable fingerprint on them.

Craft maintains that, without his mediation, the late, great works
of Stravinsky would not have come about. It is clear that Craft was
uniquely well placed to introduce Stravinsky to serialism. Craft was
not, of course, the first to have fed the composer with ideas and
materials of which Stravinsky had little previous experience, but
which in his magpie fashion he took and made his own. Through
Craft Stravinsky was also to discover then little-known Renaissance
and Baroque figures such as Gesualdo, to whose music he would
pay tribute by completing, arranging and recomposing it in *Tres
sacrae cantiones* (1957–9) and *Monumentum pro Gesualdo* (1960),
and whose traces are left elsewhere in the late work. But, as always,
in these discoveries Stravinsky saw himself. The borrowings, the
looking back, the order and formality bestowed by the serial method,
the kleptomaniac urge to take and remake, all these are familiar
facets of Stravinsky's music. This is not, for a moment, to undermine
the novelty of the late works. They were, after all, born of a desire to

reassert his modernist profile in a world in which his new work had become invisible to the young. But the Stravinskian 'attitude' remained, whatever the materials, whatever the method. We cannot know what directions Stravinsky's music would have taken had he not re-encountered the Second Viennese School via Craft. But it is also the case that in his music of the 1940s, even in *The Rake's Progress*, there is already evidence of a tendency towards the more rarefied late style, a fascination with canonical writing and refrain structures that were to become increasingly prominent features of the music after 1952. It is an extraordinary and unprecedented phenomenon that a leading composer in the evening of his creative life should have undertaken such a radical transformation of his methods and language. From this point on, in each new work, Stravinsky would experiment with something new. Stravinsky's 'serial' legacy is as heterogeneous as his 'neoclassical' one.

In 1947 Stravinsky had plundered eighteenth-century Viennese music as the principal source for his own operatic persona in *The Rake's Progress*. Now, in 1952, Stravinsky set about plundering a more recent Viennese music for his own creative purposes, mapping what he found in Schoenberg onto his own well-established ways of working.

Since the middle of 1951 Stravinsky had already been at work on a composition that grew directly out of his collaboration with Auden on the *Rake*. Auden had recently published a five-volume anthology of the *Poets of the English Language*, which he had given Stravinsky as a present. His attention was drawn by the section of 'Anonymous Lyrics and Songs', and from this he selected four lyrics that would form his Cantata for soprano and tenor soloists, a female chorus, and a pared-down ensemble of two flutes, two oboes and a cello. Guided in his choice of texts by Auden, Stravinsky began with a setting of 'The maidens came', a lyric that firmly places itself in its own time by, among other things, an invocation of 'Right mighty famus Elizabeth, our quen princis'. Given

Stravinsky's growing familiarity with Renaissance and Baroque music, this would have resonated; indeed, echoes of such music are clearly to be heard here, most notably in the Purcell-style 'Scotch snap' rhythms of the vocal setting, and also in the striking use made of strict canon by inversion. The song as a whole is characterized by its simplicity.

The composition of the Cantata was then suspended as Stravinsky made his triumphant return to Europe (his first visit since 1939) for the premiere of *The Rake's Progress* in Venice on 11 September 1951, followed by a long concert tour. It was not until the following February that he again picked up the *Poets of the English Language* to make a setting of the melancholic 'Westron winde', which may well have been in tune with his mood at the time. With its urgent cello accompaniment, it ends up sounding almost like an anxious duet for Anne and Tom discarded from a later scene of the *Rake*. But Stravinsky had come to realize that he could not carry on composing in this way. The breakthrough came with the setting for tenor of 'Tomorrow shall be my dancing day', which was to become the large, central panel of the Cantata. It is called a 'Ricecar', a title that clearly looks back to Bach and beyond. Stravinsky produces an elaborate exercise in counterpoint, where each of the eleven verses of the sixteenth-century carol takes the form of a canon, separated as in the poem by a refrain that is labelled, in the Baroque fashion, 'ritornello'. The canons are built from an eleven-note melody using just six different pitches, presented at the start in flutes and cello. The tenor then sings the four overlapping forms of this 'series' – that is, first in its basic order, then backwards ('retrograde', to use Schoenberg's term, or 'cancrizans', as Stravinsky labels it in the medieval manner), then upside down ('inversion'), and finally the upside-down version backwards ('retrograde inversion'). It is cast as a cantilena, echoing the vocal manners of *The Rake's Progress*, subconsciously prompted, maybe, by the phrase 'true love'. Underneath, the instruments sustain fifth-based harmonies and the 'Ricecar' as a whole, despite its increasing canonic complexity, maintains both a tranquil mood and a tonal focus.

Stravinsky's poetics are not hidden. Unusually, he published a detailed programme note for the occasion of the first performance in November 1952 that analyses the movement's 'serial' organization. Even more unusually, analytical annotations are retained in the published score, revealing the permutations of the canonic subject throughout 'Ricecar II'. Why did Stravinsky feel it necessary to be explicit in this way, to act as his own apologist (even if, as is likely, the text was written by Craft)? The truth must lie somewhere in his desire not only to adopt the practices of Schoenberg and Webern, but publicly and widely to be seen to be doing so. 'Since the discoveries of the Viennese School, all non-serial composers are *useless*', Boulez had declared in 1951 in his essay 'Schoenberg is Dead'. Messiaen had also begun to experiment, in his own way, with quasi-serial structures in the influential 'Mode de valeurs et d'intensités' (1949) from the *Quatre études de rythme*. On 7 May 1952 Stravinsky had attended a performance in Paris of Boulez's radical, integral serial landmark work for two pianos, *Structures Ia*, performed by Boulez and Messiaen. The venue could not have been more redolent with revolutionary significance for the senior composer: the Théâtre des Champs-Élysées. For Stravinsky, at that moment, this is where the musical future must have seemed to lie. But even at the age of 70 he was not willing to be consigned to the 'useless' pile. So the Cantata, and the commentary that surrounded it, became his own statement of radical intent.

It is fascinating, therefore, that Stravinsky completed the composition of 'Tomorrow shall be my dancing day' on 4 March 1952, four days before his reported breakdown in the California desert. There can be no independent verification of Craft's story; we have to assume it to be true in spirit, even if its primary intention is to write the storyteller directly into the history of Stravinsky's compositional development. So how are we to read the event? It seems to suggest that Stravinsky did not consider his adoption of key aspects of Viennese compositional method, by itself, to have generated anything particularly forward-looking. On the contrary, it could be argued that, now Schoenberg was dead, this was just another neoclassical move, looking back to the past. Certainly the resulting music seems little different from the interwar Stravinsky, especially the more contrapuntal examples; it still bears the hallmarks of Stravinsky's attitude to tonality familiar from so many works over the preceding 30 years. It is not the radical new music that he was hoping would speak to the young composers of the Boulez generation. Only with hindsight does it appear a small, significant step, whose implications were to be realized in later works.

And what of the expressive character of the Cantata? Clearly Auden was instrumental in moving Stravinsky towards the texts, and in some respects this project was a continuation of their successful collaboration on *The Rake's Progress*. In his programme note Stravinsky claims that he was 'persuaded by a strong desire to compose another work in which the problems of setting English words to music would reappear, but this time in a purer, non-dramatic form'. He was attracted to the selected verses, he writes, 'not only for their great beauty and their compelling syllabification, but for their construction which suggested musical construction'. (Recall his comments that the 'real subject' of *Apollo* was its 'versification'.) What could be more constructivist than a serial response? All this is as one would expect of Stravinsky, distancing himself from any meaning the texts might carry – partly, of course, because his English was still not that good and, in any case, there is evidence to show he had little understanding of this old tongue. Like the Latin of *Oedipus Rex* and the *Symphony of Psalms*, fifteenth-century English was just another distanced, dead language with which he could play games. The rhetoric of beauty, purity and construction is of a piece with the manifesto of Apollonian objectivity proclaimed in the *Poetics of Music* and elsewhere.

Yet, though he may not have understood the detail of all the texts, he would certainly have recognized their lamenting character, which spoke directly to him. Indeed, the mournful pastoral of the verses of the 'Lyke-wake dirge', which are distributed across the Cantata, are an obvious continuation of the laments of Orpheus and Anne. The lament was to appear frequently in Stravinsky's late music: in tributes to deceased friends and acquaintances (Dylan Thomas, Prince Max Egon zu Fürstenberg, President John F. Kennedy, Aldous Huxley, T. S. Eliot) as well as in his final great work, the *Requiem Canticles*. The lament came to stand as the mark of Stravinsky's late style. Or, perhaps, the lamenting that had always been a part of his music now took centre stage.

There is another text in the Cantata whose character Stravinsky must surely have registered. It was certainly remarked on by others, both at the time of its premiere and since. Whatever the Christian provenance and centuries-long history of the text, to opt to set the words mouthed by Jesus in 'Tomorrow shall be my dancing day', which proclaim that

> The Jews on me they made great suit,
> And with me made great variance;
> Because they lov'd darkness rather than light . . .

reveals, at the very least, an insensitivity on the part of the composer just a handful of years after the Holocaust. One member of the audience at the premiere of the Cantata was the Polish pianist Jakob Gimpel, a former student of Alban Berg no less, who had fled Europe for New York in 1938 and later settled in Los Angeles. He wrote a letter to the *Los Angeles Daily News* expressing his shock and offence: 'I repudiate any work that reflects a bigoted and narrow outlook.' As a musician, he was especially saddened that this 'great composer' had so shrunk in stature. The East Coast premiere a few weeks later occasioned the headline 'Lyrics of Hate' in the Jewish *Congress Weekly*.

Stravinsky did not select this text with the explicit intention of stirring up hatred, but this still does not disguise the unpalatable and incontrovertible truth that he could add anti-Semitism to his catalogue of repellent character defects that included meanness, cruelty, spitefulness, arrogance, philandering, lying and money-grubbing. This might well account for his insensitivity to the import of the words here: he was predisposed not to notice.
The pogroms and expulsion of the Jews from Russia, Poland and elsewhere in Eastern Europe were as old as Stravinsky himself. Hostility towards the Jews went with the territory of being a White Russian. In this regard Stravinsky's anti-Semitic views were hardly uncommon, and would also have been encouraged by those whose company he kept – Diaghilev pre-eminent among them. This context, however, cannot excuse his attitude. Taruskin has explored the evidence for Stravinsky the anti-Semite at length, including the exposure of hateful comments hidden in letters and private conversations.[1] Stravinsky's vehement anti-Bolshevism was wrapped up with the belief that communism was a Jewish plague and therefore 'un-Russian'. In Rome in 1930 he publicly declared his veneration of Mussolini, having two meetings with the dictator – albeit long before the consequences of fascism for Europe had become transparent. He contested his inclusion in the 1938 'Entartete Musik' exhibition in Düsseldorf by affirming to the Nazi authorities his noble, Aryan (that is, non-Jewish) roots.
He was not a Nazi sympathizer but was, for a long time, wilfully blind to what was happening in Germany, which was in part selfish opportunism, given that he relied on income from performances in Germany. And, like so many unthinking racists, his generalized anti-Semitism did not prevent him from treating individual Jewish

friends and family with respect and affection. Despite some nasty private exchanges of a racially stereotypical kind, he and his equally anti-Semitic wife, Catherine, were fond of their poet son-in-law Yuri Mandelstam, to whom Lyudmila was married in 1935 just weeks after Yuri had been baptized into the Russian Orthodox Church. (Yuri was arrested in Paris by the Gestapo in 1941 and deported to a camp in Poland, where he died in 1943. There appears to be no record of Stravinsky's reaction to his death.) Stravinsky remained close to the violinist Samuel Dushkin over many years, undertaking lengthy concert tours with him. Stravinsky even gave an inscribed copy of the Cantata score to the conductor Otto Klemperer, a friend and champion, sometime Los Angeles resident and Nazi refugee, and clearly someone he had no desire to offend. Odious though they were, Stravinsky's anti-Semitic sentiments were sporadic and ultimately more stupid and thoughtless than malevolent. The same cannot be said for his former close friends Chanel and Lifar, who continued to work in Paris throughout the Second World War, treading the path of collaboration. Even the activities of his own son Soulima were highly questionable, if selfishly motivated by the need to get concert work. Stravinsky probably did not notice the offending text in 'Tomorrow shall be my dancing day', as his surprised reaction to others' shock attests. But no rhetoric of 'beauty' and 'musical construction' can disguise the ugliness that lies beneath.

Almost as soon as he had finished the Cantata, Stravinsky began composing his next work, the Septet, which shows him entering more directly into the sphere of Schoenberg's Septet suite, the work Craft had been helping him to get to know inside out. It corresponds with the Schoenberg work not only in instrumentation but in the choice of the Baroque genre of the gigue for the last movement, and continues to engage in each of its three movements with basic aspects of the serial method. Yet the continuities with his earlier practices are also clear. The sonata-allegro first movement belongs in a line of tonally focused neoclassical works that rethink Bachian counterpoint, such as the Octet, the Sonata and the 'Dumbarton Oaks' Concerto. The ground and its treatment in the second movement are audibly derived from Bach's monumental Passacaglia in C Minor, BWV 582, though the striking presentation of the theme (a kind of *Klangfarbenmelodie* spread across all seven instruments in turn, with 'expressionistic' wide intervallic leaps) indicates a familiarity with Webern too, whose Op. 1 had been an orchestral Passacaglia and whose transcription of Bach's six-voice 'Ricercar' from *The Musical Offering* must also have played its part in the genesis of Stravinsky's own 'Passacaglia'. The closing Gigue is a highly elaborate piece of counterpoint: four fugues all told, on an eight-note subject derived from the 'Passacaglia' theme, which is inverted and retrograded, and whose forms are marked in the score. Again one wonders for whose benefit such analytical annotations are offered. No doubt Stravinsky intended them to signal his serial credentials, but equally one might think that they speak of an insecurity in his own compositional methods. They proclaim order, and a progressive kind of order at that – though, as many commentators have observed, such 'row' forms could just as well be found in Bach. So the overtly retrospective closing two string chords come as a surprise: they offer an old-style gesture of closure, but an empty gesture, a cadence in quotation marks. Suddenly the music seems to turn away from the future and look back to the final chords of *Orpheus*. The unexpected stasis here lends a strange, almost Orphic air of melancholy amid the frenetic contrapuntal activity. It is an uncanny moment, familiar yet out of place. It serves to reinforce the sense of fragility and uncertainty about the new direction Stravinsky had chosen to take. As so often before, the émigré cannot help but look over his shoulder. Tears well up in Stravinsky's eyes, just as they had done in the Mojave Desert.

11

A Citizen of the Modern World

1260 North Wetherly Drive, Los Angeles, California, 26 July 1948.
In the crammed but meticulously neat workroom of his modest,
flower-banked home on a hill overlooking Hollywood's famed
Sunset Strip, Stravinsky is writing. He usually eats breakfast on
the sunny red-tiled loggia, practically naked ('not just in shorts, but
often just wearing a handkerchief or something', says Vera). Then
he dresses, plunges into his studio, and labours away at a table that
resembles an architect's: rows of art gum erasers, each neatly labelled,
trays of pens, pencils, different colours and kinds of inks. He has
two pianos in the narrow room, a grand and an upright. The walls
are plastered with ballet programmes, sketches for ballet scenes,
drawings of himself by his friends Picasso and Cocteau, and two
large oils by his eldest son, Theodore. There are two doors between
his workroom and the light, airy, modern living room. 'When both
doors are closed, no one may enter', says Vera. 'When only the
workroom door itself is closed, I may enter, but only I.' The room
is soundproofed. Says Stravinsky, 'I cannot work where I can be
overheard.' In his personal habits he is as neat – and finicky – as
his calligraphic scores. Friends, sipping highballs, sometimes find
him methodically wiping rings left by their glasses on the table. He
likes his own drink just so. Vera measures out his Scotch highball
in the precise mixture he likes, before handing it to him.[1]

This was Stravinsky's life in Beverly Hills. But it had always
been thus, wherever he had found himself composing, wherever

The composer in his Hollywood studio, *c.* 1956.

his desk and piano had touched down, be it summer house,
temporary lodging or permanent home. A life spent in transit,
in exile, traversing Europe and America on trains, boats and
(latterly) aeroplanes found its counterbalance in the stability
of his workroom. Cocteau believed Stravinsky had inherited his
orderly habits from his teacher. 'On Rimsky's table the ink-bottles,
pen-holders and rulers revealed the bureaucrat. Stravinsky's order
is terrifying. It recalls the surgeon's instrument-case.' The desire
for order in the music, so frequently articulated, was reflected
in the professional routines of the composer.

> To see Stravinsky at Morges, or Leysin, or in Paris in his rooms
> over Pleyel's, where he lodges, is to see an animal in its shell.
> Pianos, drums, metronomes, cymbals, American pencil-
> sharpeners, desks, drums of all descriptions seem to prolong
> his person. They are like the air-pilot's rig, or the arms with
> which an insect is bedecked when we see it in the cinema
> magnified a thousand times, at pairing time.[2]

Craft repeats the surgical metaphor in his description of the composer's Los Angeles studio:

> I.S. exercises for nearly an hour before breakfast, including 15 minutes of hatha yogi head-stands. His breakfast consists of espresso and two raw eggs, swallowed in single gulps. After it, he takes me to his *sanctum sanctorum* and plays his Mass and as much as he has composed of the first scene of the *Rake*. His piano is a tacky-sounding and out-of-tune upright dampened with felt. A plywood board is attached to its music rack, and quarto-size strips of thick manila paper are clipped to it. All the staves are drawn with his styluses [the self-styled 'Stravigor', an adjustable wheeled rastrum that Stravinsky had attempted to patent in 1911, and which he used to rule his musical staves]. To the side of the piano is a kind of surgeon's operating table . . . [31 July 1948][3]

It was in this ordered environment that Stravinsky's most overtly ordered music was written. 'I have tremendous respect for the discipline imposed on the twelve-tone man. It is a discipline that you find nowhere else', he told the *New York Herald Tribune* at the end of 1952.

Robert Craft's testimony, so often quoted in this book, is a documentary resource of unmatched significance. A graduate of the Juilliard School, Craft had been an admirer of Stravinsky's music since the age of twelve. The two entered into correspondence in 1944 and finally met face-to-face on 31 March 1948 at the elegant Raleigh Hotel in Washington, DC, at the same moment as Auden arrived to hand over the completed libretto of *The Rake's Progress*. Craft obviously made a reasonable impression, though unsurprisingly he recalls being rather tongue-tied. By 30 July he had gone to stay with the Stravinskys at North Wetherly Drive and from then on spent increasing periods of time in their company. In 1949 Stravinsky invited Craft to spend the summer with him in California in order to sort and catalogue his manuscripts, recently arrived from Paris, where they had been languishing since before the war. Craft also advised the composer on Auden's text for the *Rake*, reading aloud, 'over and over and at varying speeds, the lines of whichever aria, recitative or ensemble he was about to set to music'. From then on, until the composer's death over twenty years later, Craft was Stravinsky's Achates, as he described himself (after Aeneas' faithful friend in Virgil's *Aeneid*), remaining virtually continuously at the composer's side, sharing his home and hotel suites with him, his wife and their many famous visitors. There is hardly a photograph of Stravinsky in his later years, in both professional and social settings, in which Craft does not also appear somewhere. By the end Craft was far closer to Stravinsky than any of his children; arguably, given their uniquely intimate musical relationship, he had access to the composer that even his wife could not match.

This Beverly Hills *ménage à trois* is an extraordinary phenomenon about which much has been written and still more speculated. Above all else, Craft's presence among the Stravinskys afforded him (and therefore us) unprecedented access to the minutiae of the composer's later life. Stravinsky's daily routines, his compositional habits, his conversations, all these were noted by Craft in his diaries and published soon after the composer's death. Like any such documents, these diaries are as much about the observer as the observed, and despite external corroboration of some of the detail, it remains difficult to evaluate their veracity since there were no other witnesses aside from Vera. It is only natural that Craft should have written himself a central part in the story, even though, in the process of recording (and often rewriting) his experiences, he confesses that he discovered an 'alter ego' of which he was 'not especially fond'. Over time, the alter ego has become virtually indistinguishable from the self.

Craft was Stravinsky's factotum. He was his assistant in
all things musical. He was the trusted conductor of his music,
including significant premieres. He was the resident advisor
in matters pertaining to the English language. He was a valued
intermediary not only with musicians and their representatives
but, at times, with Stravinsky's own family. Indeed, he was a filial
substitute. He even became Stravinsky's confessor. Perhaps most
importantly, Craft was the last in a line of exegetes that Stravinsky
always seemed to require: the expounder, the public interpreter of
scripture. Arthur Lourié, Jacques Rivière, Boris de Schloezer, Pierre
Souvtchinsky, among others, had all preceded Craft: variously
mouthpieces, ghostwriters, hagiographers, apologists, *éminences
grises*, who could present the composer to the world in the way he
wished to be seen.[4] Spin doctors all, *avant la lettre*. This was Craft's
role too, embraced to a hubristic degree. (On 7 April 1948, just a
week after having met Stravinsky for the first time, he observed:
'I know the Symphony in C better than Mr S. does.') Aside from
the diaries, there are edited volumes of photographs, documents,
letters and reminiscences. And then there is the invaluable series
of late *Conversations* with Stravinsky, published over a ten-year
period from 1959. Invaluable but, as is often noted, untrustworthy.
In part, this was inevitable, as Craft was inviting Stravinsky to review
his entire life, and either his memory played tricks, or else he chose
(as was his wont) to reinvent the past to suit present purposes. The
Conversations are billed a collaboration. Craft's role was far more
than mere scribe: he wrote the books; he shaped them; he put
words into Stravinsky's mouth. He asserts he remained faithful
to the substance of the composer's thoughts, even though the
language is largely Craft's own. But as with other of Stravinsky's
dicta – the *Autobiography*, the *Poetics*, even the recorded legacy
– the authenticity of the *Conversations* can never be assumed.

What cannot be denied is the importance of Craft to Stravinsky.
Stravinsky relied on Craft's musical skills in so many ways. Walsh is

right to assert that in later years, Stravinsky could hardly have functioned on tour without Craft's help, preparing orchestras for the maestro, supervising recording sessions, and so on.[5] And without Craft the late serial works would not have emerged as they did. Hard though it is to imagine, had it not been for Craft, Stravinsky may never have overcome his creative crisis and would simply have ceased composing at all.

The rebirth of Stravinsky's language that was taking place with Craft's support nearly became embodied in the subject-matter of a work. In 1950 Auden had introduced Stravinsky to the poetry of Dylan Thomas, and in 1952 the two were approached to collaborate on a film project based on a scene from the *Odyssey*, but it foundered for lack of money. They finally met in Boston in 1953. 'As soon as I saw him I knew that the only thing to do was to love him.' Thomas had an idea for an opera about 'the rediscovery of our planet following an atomic misadventure. There would be a re-creation of language.' It is obvious that this would have resonated with Stravinsky's own situation at the time. But the project was never even begun. Thomas died on 9 November in New York. 'All I could do was cry', recalled Stravinsky. Early the following year he began composing *In memoriam Dylan Thomas* using Thomas's memorial poem to his own father, 'Do not go gentle into that good night'. Its villanelle form gave Stravinsky the kind of refrain structure he had used so often before, while the sentiments of the poet raging against the dying of the light echoed Stravinsky's rare admission of emotion at the death of a man he had, in fact, met only once. Many of Stravinsky's late works may seem dry, severe, all too orderly (like his desk); in *In memoriam* Stravinsky's *espressivo* manner re-emerges for the first time since *The Rake's Progress*. The touching setting of the text for tenor and string quartet is framed by an instrumental prelude and postlude for trombone quartet and string quartet, each named a 'dirge-canon'. Reflecting on Thomas's desire for the 're-creation of language', Stravinsky produced his first genuinely serial work. Its five-note chromatic set generates all the pitch material. The serial transformations, where each repetition is always the same yet always different, capture a sense of mourning, as the music continually turns back in on itself. The steady tread of the repeated notes and the falling chromatic lines of lament in the dirge-canons allude to ceremonial traditions from Gabrieli's Venice that were shortly to take on a greater significance for Stravinsky, and certainly carry resonances of *Orpheus*. This music has a desolate dignity. Stravinsky's serial method may have been new, but the music's lamenting character reaches deep into his musical and personal history.

The remaining years of Stravinsky's active creative life were dominated by the production of large-scale sacred choral works on biblical texts (by way of medieval English mystery plays in the case of *The Flood*, a 'musical play' for television) and small-scale memorial pieces. But composition was often interrupted by the demands of a gruelling schedule of touring and recording that took the composer not only the length and breadth of North America and across Europe, but to Japan, South America, North and Southern Africa, Israel, New Zealand and Australia. For a man in his late seventies, increasingly troubled by bouts of ill health and with a serious blood condition, it was a work-scheme that bordered on madness. In 1956 he had already suffered a serious stroke that had necessitated an enforced five-week confinement in a Munich hospital and which had disrupted the composition of *Agon*. But this was not going to force him into retirement. Igor Stravinsky was by now a major global commodity, and the composer was keen to maximize the income from his own name. He had become arguably the first true celebrity composer. He was addicted to the attention it brought him.

Others, too, were eager to exploit the 'idea' of Igor Stravinsky. In 1945 Stravinsky's music had been presented in Paris as a symbol of liberty. By the mid-1940s, having taken U.S. citizenship, Stravinsky was reinvented as an American. In 1948 *Time* magazine reported that he liked to be known as a 'California composer', while the fifth edition of *Grove's Dictionary of Music and Musicians* (published in 1954) defined him as an 'American composer of Russian origin'. In 1952 the composer Nicolas Nabokov, a friend and fellow Russian émigré, mounted a festival of twentieth-century music in Paris under the title *L'Oeuvre du xxe siècle*. Nabokov was secretary-general of the Congress for Cultural Freedom, an organization funded covertly by the CIA as just one strand of its involvement with anti-Communist groups in post-war Europe, and this musical showcase was organized with the explicit purpose of presenting 'the products of free minds in a free world'.[6] For Nabokov, Stravinsky's neoclassicism represented renewal, and so it came about that the Symphony in C, one of Stravinsky's most apparently 'neutral' works, was drawn into the ideological conflicts of the Cold War. To the extent that Stravinsky realized what was going on, and to the extent that he remained vehemently opposed to Stalin's regime, he became a willing participant in this cultural propaganda war. That the name of Stravinsky continued to be of great value in the highest American political circles was confirmed by that fact that, in early 1962, in the year of his eightieth birthday, Stravinsky and Vera were invited to dine at the White House by Jacqueline Kennedy. Neither she nor the president, it would seem, had much interest in Stravinsky's music. Stravinsky himself was well aware of the usefulness to them of this famous Russian turned American.

For their part, having left him out in the cold for so long, the Soviets gradually took more interest in Stravinsky and his music. In a glorious symmetry, at the end of the same year in which he had been welcomed into the heart of American power, Stravinsky made his first return to Russia in nearly half a century, and was summoned to the Kremlin to meet Nikita Khrushchev, chairman of the Council of Ministers and de facto premier of the USSR.

Igor and Vera Stravinsky arriving in Moscow, 21 September 1962.

Straddling the divided world as no diplomat could, Igor Stravinsky
had become a piece of priceless Cold War capital. It is a remarkable
illustration of what his name had come to represent, quite
independently of the man himself or, for that matter, of the music
he wrote. For Stravinsky himself, the three-week tour of the Soviet
Union was a powerful homecoming. He conducted in Moscow
and Leningrad; he appeared on Soviet television; he attended a
Stravinsky exhibition; he met composers, musicians and relatives;
he visited Kryukov Canal (though not his childhood apartment)
and was thwarted only in his wish to return to Ustilug. At a dinner
organized in Moscow by the Minister of Culture, Yekaterina
Furtseva, Stravinsky gave an emotional speech: 'A man has one
birthplace, one fatherland, one country – he *can* have only one
country – and the place of his birth is the most important factor
in his life.' This was an extraordinary confession for one who had,

over so many decades, done his utmost to deny the significance of his native culture. Yet, even in California, Russian was still the domestic language, the language of his thoughts; sentimental objects from Russia were scattered about his studio. Craft's observation of the change in Stravinsky's nature while on Russian soil is deeply touching. 'I.S. does regret his uprooting and exile more than anything else in his life'.

> Just five years ago [1957], in Baden-Baden, he flew into a rage on hearing the news of Sputnik, forbidding us even to mention the Russian achievement. Was the power of this jealous hatred, the result of the Mother Country's deprived love, responsible for his at times too conspicuous 'Western sophistication', in the sense that the latter became a weapon to prove his superiority, and that of other cultures, to the Russia which failed to recognize his genius? I am certain of only one thing: that to be recognized and acclaimed as a Russian in Russia, and to be performed here, has meant more to him than anything else in the years I have known him.[7]

The return to Russia confronted Stravinsky directly with the reality of the state of exile in which he had lived most his life and which had coloured virtually his entire creative output.

Back in the U.S., as he continued to develop and refine his serial technique, Stravinsky had had another beloved city on his mind: Venice. Here were premiered both the *Canticum Sacrum ad honorem Sancti Marci nominis* (St Mark's Basilica, 1956) and *Threni: id est Lamentationes Jeremiae Prophetae* (Scuole Grande di San Rocco, 1958). Echoes of the music of that city (Gabrieli and Monteverdi most notably) find their way into the manner and shape of the works. Like the *Symphony of Psalms*, their Latin texts are taken from the Vulgate Bible; like the *Psalms* they are liturgies. These two works, along with *Agon*, which was completed between them,

are Stravinsky's only major late compositions that, in part
or in whole, deploy twelve-note rows of a (crudely speaking)
Schoenbergian or Webernian kind. Strikingly they are also among
the most ritualized of his late works, the method lending them
a hieratic intensity. Yet across them – in their chanting, their
processionals, their repetitions, their use of pedal points and so
on – echo the laments and rituals of so many of his earlier works.

The most exceptional work of Stravinsky's late years is a short
'concerto' for piano and orchestra entitled *Movements*, started in
1958 and completed at the end of July 1959. The name refers,
obviously, to the fact the work is in five separate movements,
connected by four short 'interludes' in which the piano is silent
and which anticipate the tempo of the subsequent movement. But
it also suggests the rhythmic movements of points of sound about
the orchestra, the movement across the music's five distinct tempos,
and perhaps also the rotation of the twelve-note row from which
the piece is built. It might even imply the imaginary presence of
moving bodies, a kind of abstract drama that was in fact to be
realized a few years later when Balanchine decided to choreograph
the work. But such a bland description does little to prepare the
listener for music which, on first hearing, is entirely unexpected,
offering a version of the sound-world of his young, avant-garde
contemporaries in Paris and Darmstadt. That the most famous
composer of his day was willing to rethink his musical language so
radically in order to form a rapprochement with the experiments
of men 50 years his junior is both unprecedented as well as an
indication of his ongoing fear of being considered *démodé*. The
shadow of Webern is cast strongly over the work, but as heard
through younger ears – say, the pointillistic pianism of Boulez's
Structures Ia, or the fragmentation and instrumental grouping
of Boulez's *Le Marteau sans maître*, or the play of speeds in
Stockhausen's *Zeitmasse*, the last two of which Craft had recorded
in 1958. Even the presentation of the score, where the staves vanish

when not required, imitates the style of the 'house' publisher of the European avant-garde, Universal Edition. Stravinsky is here rethinking his own musical experiences, as he had done so often before; this greatest of all musical magpies, even in his late seventies, is attempting to refashion what he discovers around him and make it his own. Closer listening does reveal Stravinskian thumbprints, notably the characteristic voicing of chords, and structures built from hidden repetitions of carefully coloured blocks, as if *Movements* were some sort of scattered memory of the *Symphonies of Wind Instruments*. To the extent that this fragmentation is a sign of the 'lateness' of this work, it fits the narrative of Stravinsky's final decades. Equally its ongoing quest after new forms of order is typical. But in fact it is just as fruitful to evaluate *Movements* as a unique moment in Stravinsky's output, a late flowering of his ever-youthful imagination, of his desire always to invent, to make anew.

Stravinsky's last major work is also the greatest achievement of his serial years. The *Requiem Canticles* was begun in Los Angeles in March 1965, interrupted many times by yet more extensive concert and recording activity in America and Europe – extraordinary for a man in his eighties who was becoming increasingly frail – and completed on 13 August 1966. Craft conducted the first performance in October at Princeton University. Commissioned as an instrumental work in memory of a benefactress to that university, this setting for orchestra, chorus and soloists of fragments of the Latin requiem mass text must surely have been motivated, in part at least, by the composer's knowledge that his own life was entering its final phase. After the Princeton premiere, the university president Robert F. Goheen expressed his hope that Princeton would be able to welcome the composer again. 'I am a very old man and that is unlikely', was Stravinsky's morbid response. Vera later told Craft that '*he* and *we* knew he was writing it for himself ', and in her letter of instruction for Stravinsky's funeral, written a year before his death, she specified that she wished this work to be performed in his memory. What Stravinsky's wish was with regard to the venue, shape and musical content of his funeral is not known, as he vehemently refused to discuss it. But there is nothing about the work itself that is at all morbid, even though it has the undeniable character of a late work. André Boucourechliev perfectly captures its mood when he writes that the *Requiem Canticles* are memories, 'as though in his old age the composer were casting a keen glance over the past, reviewing and evoking all his music'.[8]

Stravinsky had written this piece many times before. He had spent his life looking back, lamenting. The *Requiem Canticles* is awash with echoes of earlier works. But what is most striking is its serenity. It is elegiac, certainly, but also devotional. In its closing moments this music has no sense of a raging against the dying of the light, nor even of resignation, but of peace, of a coming-to-terms with the inevitability of death. Despite the size of the forces deployed here, this is no Verdian requiem but an intimate, chamber piece. The representation of the day of wrath ('Dies irae') and the trumpets' call to judgement ('Tuba mirum') sit on the borderland between awe and mockery as if the spirit of Petruhska were still present, thumbing his nose at death itself. The twelve-note method has now been fully assimilated and transformed into something entirely Stravinsky's own, where music and method are as one. The rotational arrays that generate the chords of the 'Postlude' ('chords of death', Craft calls them) give the sense of order that had been Stravinsky's lifelong pursuit, his lifelong obsession, but they also enable a ritualized expression to speak through. The celesta, tubular bells and vibraphone that chime slowly and regularly are funeral bells, but with an inner exuberance, just like the wedding bells at the end of *Les Noces*. 'Bells are always pealing in Russian music and bells are always pealing in the music of the singer's son', write Louis Andriessen and Elmer Schönberger.[9] This is a Proustian moment of involuntary memory. The bells at the close of the *Requiem Canticles* transport Stravinsky joyfully back to the bells of St Petersburg, where he had begun. Time is transcended. The bells ring out into infinity.

It was not Stravinsky's last word. As he was putting the final touches to the *Requiem* he began a delightful setting of Edward Lear's nonsense poem *The Owl and the Pussycat*, for singer and a single line on the piano. A piece of two-part counterpoint, it almost seems to poke fun at the twelve-note method, as the owl and the pussycat chase each other's musical tails throughout. One of Stravinsky's Russian nonsense songs from the years of the First World War has been transplanted to the U.S. West Coast. It is also perhaps a tender, teasing, cartoon portrait of himself and Vera, to whom it is dedicated. There is something fitting in the fact that it is this playful vignette and not the *Requiem Canticles* that should be Stravinsky's final original composition, his comic epilogue. Like Baba at the end of *The Rake's Progress*, here is Stravinsky, faced with his own end, stepping up to the footlights and grinning out at the audience, revealing his fine array of white teeth, but with eyes hidden behind a pair of dark glasses, in just the same enigmatic way he had done in so many photographs from his American life.

Stravinsky's closing years were dogged by poor health and family feuds. There were unsuccessful attempts to start new works, and he made transcriptions of Bach and Hugo Wolf (according to Craft, because he 'wanted to say something about death and felt that he could not compose anything of his own'). Travel became increasingly difficult. He persisted with his by now highly lucrative podium appearances, but these too eventually came to an end in Toronto in May 1967 with a performance of the *Pulcinella* suite. The last performance of his own music he attended was appropriately of the work and in the city that had first secured his worldwide reputation as a modernist: *The Rite of Spring* in Paris, in Béjart's notorious animalistic choreography. In another fortuitous closing of the circle, the last years of this Art Deco composer par excellence were spent in New York City, principally in an apartment in the Art Deco Essex House overlooking the southern edge of Central Park. Designed by Frank Grad and opened in 1931, the building's severe exterior hid an interior opulence. Every day Stravinsky and Vera would have been reminded of the glories of the achievements of the Art Deco style as they travelled up and down to their condominium in an elevator whose most glorious brass doors of exotic floral design set in walls of black marble resonated back over half a century to the first opulent designs for the Ballets Russes. And in a final gesture befitting one who had spent a life in transit, the life of an émigré, just a week before his death Stravinsky – 'fragile as a silk thread, tough as a steel wire', in the words of Theodore and Denise Stravinsky – moved to a grand apartment on Fifth Avenue, once again overlooking Central Park. He passed away there in the early hours of 6 April 1971, aged 88. Who, if anyone, was with him at the moment he died is unclear; as with his life, the facts surrounding Stravinsky's death are the subject of multiple, contradictory accounts. Craft writes himself into the deathbed scene; others record it differently. But it was Vera who called for the mirrors to be covered in an act of superstition of which Stravinsky would no doubt have approved. Vera outlived Igor by another decade, becoming a familiar lone figure, or on the arm of Craft, walking the sidewalks of the affluent Upper East Side. She died on 17 September 1982 in her 93rd year, in the room in which her husband had died, 100 years after his birth. She is laid to rest next to him on the cemetery island of San Michele in Venice, just metres from the impresario who had engineered their first meeting in Paris some 61 years before.

Stravinsky conducting the Warsaw Philharmonic Orchestra, Warsaw, 29 May 1965.

Postlude: Stravinsky Remains

Wednesday 29 May 2013, Théâtre des Champs-Élysées, avenue Montaigne. All fashionable Paris is here. Politicians, diplomats, business people and the elite of the musical and dance worlds throng the pavement outside the theatre. Just a few metres further down the avenue towards the Place de l'Alma is parked a police van. Three agents of the Police Nationale – two in uniform, one in plain clothes – lean casually against its open door, smoking. Are they expecting a riot? Well, yes, but a protest by La Manif Pour Tous against plans for equal marriage occasioned by the presence of so many key members of the socialist government rather than directly by the ballet about to be performed. With rather delicious echoes of the premiere, violent scuffles break out in the street. The minister responsible for the police, the minister of the interior and future prime minister Manuel Valls, is among the crowd, along with his violinist wife, Anne Gravoin, herself the granddaughter of an émigré from Stalin's Soviet Union. So too is Aurélie Filippetti, the minister of culture, and her predecessor, Jack Lang. The president of the French Republic is represented by his partner, Valérie Trierweiler. Both the Swiss and Russian ambassadors are present, on behalf of the two countries in which the work they are about to see was principally conceived and composed. And the families of some of the original protagonists have also flown over from the u.s. to witness this special event, most notably the composer's 67-year-old grandson John Stravinsky and the choreographer's 93-year-old daughter Tamara Nijinsky.

A lone bassoonist called Igor from the Mariinsky Theatre Orchestra emerges from the main entrance and stands on the top step below the theatre's canopy emblazoned with its name in freshly restored gilt lettering. High in the instrument's register a melody emerges, a distorted folk tune, the sounds of 'nature renewing itself', sounds now familiar the world over but which were once considered so strange and unnatural. The rain has held off, so a good size crowd is gathering to watch a well-publicized 'flash mob' take place amid the geometrical patterns taped onto the *parvis*. A 'mash up' of fragments of *Le Sacre du printemps* is projected from speakers, as dancers from conservatoires across the city of Paris start to move in serried ranks, while two youths declaim Stravinsky's essay 'Ce que j'ai voulu exprimé dans *Le Sacre du printemps*', published this day exactly 100 years earlier. Competing cries of 'bravo!' and 'boo!' are heard from among the mob. This is the riot at the *Rite*, equally well orchestrated, it would seem, as the celebrated first-night commotion, drawing attention once again to Diaghilev's famous creation ahead of its centenary performance.

Scandal still shadows this work. Just two days earlier, *Le Monde* has published an open letter from Tamara Nijinsky. First, she expresses her pleasure that the Théâtre is honouring the *Rite* with four performances. But it is the first time she will have attended a performance of the 'so-called "original" version' as reconstituted in 1987 by Hodson and Archer. It will also be the first time that the Nijinsky successors will have received any authors' rights. 'I bring these facts to your attention', she writes, 'in our wish to make public the injustice which has been done for over a quarter of a century.' Just as it did throughout the life of the composer of the music that accompanies the ballet, the ugly noise of argument over money and rights threatens to drown out the sound of art. '*À tous, bon centenaire du "Sacre du printemps"*.'[1] Is her valedictory gesture genuine or ironic? As so often before with those involved with this piece, it is hard to tell.

The well-dressed audience makes its way inside, sweeping up the plush red carpets of the Art Deco stairways. Much Russian can be heard amid the international babble of voices. The original seasons of the Ballets Russes had been supported by, among others, the Petersburg-born *reine de Paris*, Misia Edwards, later Sert. Today it is Gazprom, the $100-billion global energy company in which the Russian Federation has a majority shareholding, which is sponsoring the performance. Once in their seats, waiting expectantly for the arrival in the pit of maestro Valery Gergiev, the public is treated to a lengthy speech from Michel Franck, the theatre's manager and artistic director, successor to the man whose vision brought about the building of the theatre in the first place, Gabriel Astruc. This great ballet may have been the product of the Russian imagination, overseen by a Russian impresario, premiered by Russian musicians and dancers, but its success is ineluctably linked to Paris. Even today, asserts Franck, *Le Sacre* belongs to Paris. And, as if to demonstrate that the *snobisme* so evident in the aristocratic ladies of the 16th arrondissement who attended the premiere is still alive and well, he calls all present, '*invités et non-invités*', to partake of a glass of champagne in the interval.

The chandelier in the centre of Maurice Denis's glorious dome dims, and Igor Gorbunov once again begins his famous solo. Roerich's curtain rises to reveal the mysterious hill, and the ghost of Nijinsky provokes the Mariinsky dancers to jerk into life once more. This time there are no calls for doctor or dentist. The performance is received in rapt silence and concludes with rapturous applause. Following the interval, the music is repeated, now with a new choreography from the German Sasha Waltz, making reference to a century of dancing the work, from Nijinsky to Bausch, at the end of which the Chosen One is killed slowly and spectacularly by a golden dagger descending from the flies. The Paris *claqueurs* are there in good number to boo, as is their wont, while the rest try to drown them out with their clapping and cheering, which continue for a very long time. Finally, as the audience steps out onto the now dark avenue Montaigne, they see the facade of the Théâtre des Champs-Élysées illuminated by the searchlight at the top of the Eiffel Tower, just as it had been on the evening of its inauguration on 5 April 1913. A hundred years on, this theatre and this work remain at the centre of the City of Light.

Stravinsky demeure. Stravinsky remains. So wrote Pierre Boulez in a celebrated essay first published in 1951, in which he performed a spectacular analysis of *The Rite of Spring* in order to demonstrate how rhythm acts as the music's principal structural agent but which, equally, tells the reader a great deal about Boulez's own compositional priorities.[2] Boulez was neither the first nor the last to play the magpie Igor Stravinsky at his own game and plunder the music for his own purposes. 'Everyone, after all, has been influenced by Stravinsky', wrote the Dutch composer Louis Andriessen in 1983. 'The true influence of Stravinsky keeps beginning all over again.'[3] That influence can clearly be traced in the impact the music had on those who were at the early ballet premieres right through to the present. There are subtle echoes in Debussy and Ravel and stronger allusions in George Antheil and Edgard Varèse. There are 'all those little *Sacres* composed between 1920 and 1940 in the Soviet Union, Poland, Hungary, up to and including the Netherlands: umpa, umpa-pa, um, strings thumping away, never enough time-signature changes'.[4] There is a post-First World War French Stravinskianism led by Poulenc, followed by the other members of Les Six, whose knowledge of Stravinsky is so intimate that it can sometimes sound like direct quotation. There are the post-Second World War Boston neoclassicists, named the 'Stravinsky school' by Aaron Copland, himself a member, and including Arthur Berger, Leonard Bernstein, Irving Fine and Harold Shapero. There is an avant-garde line of composers who look to the primitive, the ritualistic and the mythic in Stravinsky and turn it to their own purposes, from Olivier Messiaen and Harrison Birtwistle to Conlon Nancarrow and Elliott Carter. There are the American minimalists, such as Steve Reich and John Adams, who still love to live inside a Stravinskian harmonic world, and their followers, such as Michael Torke and Nico Muhly, who love to fuse Stravinsky with rock and pop. And then there are the sounds of Stravinsky from *The Firebird* onwards that echo across countless film scores. Even for the young composer setting out on a career today, Stravinsky is impossible to ignore. Uniquely, perhaps, among progressive composers of the twentieth century, Stravinsky remains.

As the celebrations in Paris on 29 May 2013 reveal, Stravinsky's music – as well as the myths that surround it – lives on in the imagination of the wider public too. Never has the anniversary of the premiere of a single work been feted in this way before. During his lifetime Stravinsky and his associates traded on the *Rite* to turn Stravinsky into a celebrity named 'Stravinsky', an eminently saleable commodity. If anything, since the composer's death, the presence of Stravinsky's music in concert halls, opera houses and ballet theatres has grown all the stronger. Stravinsky continues to sell. But why? The music is, certainly, by turn, colourful and dynamic; active and contemplative; it tells good stories; it innovates; it is always beautifully crafted. But this is true of much other music of the twentieth century too. Stravinsky's was a particular life lived in the shadow of wars, revolution, illness and death; an itinerant life framed by a love of sex, whisky, money and fashion; a creative life full of extraordinary encounters with musicians, poets, painters, dancers, directors and impresarios – all so much potentially mouth-watering material for a biographer. Yet while this shaped the music, the music never directly represents any of it. Rather, like the work of his two great contemporaries in art and poetry, Picasso and Eliot, whose creative paths all parallel one another in fascinating ways, the changing course of Stravinsky's music subtly and vicariously registers the vicissitudes of the century through which the man lived. From memories of pre-revolutionary Russia to the losses of wartime Switzerland, from the exuberance of France in the Roaring Twenties to the stability of America late in life, the music charts his shifts in perspective. Certainly, ever the opportunist, with one eye always on where his next commission might come from, he reacted quickly to changing fashions. His old friend Diaghilev had taught him well. But there is more to it than this. The music's power is achieved by standing back from the changing world, reflecting on it, commenting on it. It can make one laugh; it can make one weep; it can overwhelm. Even when espousing the simplest-seeming of materials, as in *Apollo*, the music can suddenly take a surprising turn and lead the listener into darker terrain. It speaks profoundly of a modern life of literal and metaphorical exile with all its attendant sorrows. It speaks of the twentieth century.

Where, then, is the 'real' Stravinsky? As Cocteau discovered early on, the facts of this life as documented by a biographer can only represent a world of appearances, so many masks worn by this 'master conjuror', in Adorno's phrase, this inveterate liar, this riddle wrapped in a mystery inside an enigma. The closer one looks, the more any sense of the real seems to retreat from one's grasp. Did anyone, will anyone ever get his or her hands on the real Igor Fyodorovich Stravinsky? All that is left is the music, and to my ears, that is where I find the fragile, human, all too human Stravinsky, lurking below the surface, from where he speaks to me, quietly, movingly. That is where Stravinsky remains.

References

Preface: Finding Igor

1 Rett Ertl and Rick Hibberd, *The Art of the Russian Matryoshka* (Boulder, CO, 2004), p. 3.
2 Ibid., p. 8.

Prelude: How Stravinsky Became 'Stravinsky'

1 Richard Wagner, *Beethoven* (Leipzig, 1870), p. 26; trans. by Scott Burnham in *Beethoven Hero* (Princeton, NJ, 1995), p. 155.
2 Robert Craft, *Stravinsky: Chronicle of a Friendship* (revd and expanded edn, Nashville, TN, 1994), p. 547.
3 From the diary of Johann Carl Rosenbaum; quoted in David Wyn Jones, *The Life of Beethoven* (Cambridge, 1998), p. 181.

1 A Son of St Petersburg

1 Igor Stravinsky and Robert Craft, *Expositions and Developments* (London, 1962, reprinted 1981), p. 51.
2 Tamara Levitz's discussion of death in Stravinsky is especially revealing: see *Modernist Mysteries: Perséphone* (New York, 2012), especially 'Stravinsky's Purgatory', in chapter Seven, pp. 518–60.
3 Orlando Figes, *Natasha's Dance: A Cultural History of Russia* (London, 2002), pp. 10, 7.
4 Ibid., pp. 13, 44–5.

5 'Lyubite muzïku!', *Komsomol'skaya Pravda* (27 September 1962), quoted in Richard Taruskin, *Stravinsky and the Russian Traditions: A Biography of the Works through 'Mavra'* (Oxford, 1996), p. 13.
6 Figes, *Natasha's Dance*, p. 53.
7 Stravinsky and Craft, *Expositions and Developments*, p. 36.
8 For extensive discussion of the sources, composition, revision and reception of the symphony, including facsimiles of sketches, see Taruskin, *Stravinsky and the Russian Traditions*, pp. 171–233.
9 Ibid., p. 222.

2 Russian Ballets

1 Quoted in Sjeng Scheijen, *Diaghilev: A Life*, trans. Jane Hedley-Prôle and S. J. Leinbach (London, 2009), p. 74.
2 Igor Stravinsky, 'The Diaghilev I Knew', *Atlantic Monthly*, CXCII/5 (November 1953), pp. 33–6.
3 See Scheijen, *Diaghilev*, pp. 98–101.
4 Ibid., p. 167.
5 Henri Ghéon, writing in the *Nouvelle revue française* (1910), quoted in Stephen Walsh, *Igor Stravinsky: A Creative Spring. Russia and France, 1882–1934* (London, 2000), p. 143.
6 Boris Asaf 'yev, *A Book about Stravinsky*, trans. Richard F. French (Ann Arbor, MI, 1982), p. 19; first published in Leningrad in 1929 as *Kniga o Stravinskom* under Asaf 'yev's nom de plume, Igor Glebov.

3 Portrait of a Scandal

1 Jean Cocteau, 'Cock and Harlequin', in *A Call to Order*, trans. Rollo H. Myers (New York, 1974), pp. 42–3.
2 Ibid., p. 45.
3 P. Drevliansky, *Belorusskie narodnie predaniya* [Belarusian Folk Traditions] (1846), quoted and trans. in Paul Griffiths and Edmund Griffiths, 'The Shaman, the Sage and the Sacrificial Victim – and Nicholas Roerich's Part in it All', in *Avatar of Modernity: 'The Rite of*

Spring' Reconsidered, ed. Hermann Danuser and Heidy Zimmermann (London, 2013), p. 50.

4 On the musical sources for the *Rite*, see Richard Taruskin, *Stravinsky and the Russian Traditions: A Biography of the Works through 'Mavra'* (Oxford, 1996), pp. 891–923.

5 A fuller comparison is made in Jonathan Cross, 'Rewriting the *Rite*: Creative Responses to *Le Sacre du printemps*', in *Avatar of Modernity*, ed. Danuser and Zimmermann, pp. 199–201.

4 A First Exile: Switzerland, War and Revolution

1 Eric Walter White, *Stravinsky: The Composer and his Works* (2nd edn, London, 1979), pp. 234–5.

2 Stephen Walsh, *The Music of Stravinsky* (Oxford, 1988), p. 86.

3 Richard Taruskin, *Stravinsky and the Russian Traditions: A Biography of the Works through 'Mavra'* (Oxford, 1996), pp. 1298–9.

4 Igor Stravinsky, *An Autobiography (1903–1934)* (London, 1990, originally published in French as *Chroniques de ma vie*, Paris, 1935), p. 70. The English translation was first published in 1936 (no translator given).

5 Roman Vlad, *Stravinsky*, trans. Frederick and Ann Fuller (3rd paperback edn, London, 1985), p. 72.

5 A Creative Epiphany: Parisian Style and Neoclassicism

1 Romain Rolland, *Journal des années de guerre* (entry for 26 September 1914), trans. and cited in Stephen Walsh, *Igor Stravinsky: A Creative Spring. Russia and France, 1882–1934* (London, 2000), p. 244.

2 Quoted in *Igor and Vera Stravinsky: A Photograph Album, 1921–1971* (London, 1982), p. 89.

3 Jean Cocteau, 'The Latest Stravinsky', *La Revue musicale* (1 December 1923); trans. Bridget Behrmann and Tamara Levitz, in *Stravinsky and His World*, ed. Tamara Levitz (Princeton, NJ, 2013), p. 43.

4 Mary E. Davis, 'Chanel, Stravinsky, and Musical Chic', *Fashion Theory*, x/4 (2006), pp. 452, 434–6. See also Mary E. Davis, *Classic*

Chic: Music, Fashion and Modernism (Berkeley, CA, 2006), especially chapter Six.

5 Chris Greenhalgh, *Coco and Igor* (London, 2002); Greenhalgh also wrote the screenplay for *Coco Chanel and Igor Stravinsky* (2009), directed by Jan Kounen.

6 Robert Craft, *Stravinsky: Glimpses of a Life* (New York, 1992), p. 13.

7 Robert Craft, 'Amorous Augmentations', in *Stravinsky: Discoveries and Memories* (n.p., 2013), p. 163.

8 Ibid., p. 172.

9 Théodore and Denise Strawinsky, *Au coeur du Foyer: Catherine et Igor Strawinsky, 1906–1940* (Borg-la-Reine, 1998), p. 138 (my translation).

10 Richard Taruskin, *Stravinsky and the Russian Traditions: A Biography of the Works through 'Mavra'* (Oxford, 1996), pp. 1648, 1675. Taruskin paraphrases Stravinsky's words from an interview in *Komsomol'skaya pravda* (27 September 1962).

11 Davis, 'Chanel, Stravinsky, and Musical Chic', p. 432.

12 Reproduced as Ex. 13.4 in Charlotte Benton, Tim Benton and Ghislaine Wood, eds, *Art Deco, 1910–1939* (London, 2003), p. 159.

13 See Valerie Mendes, 'Art Deco Fashion', in *Art Deco*, ed. Benton et al., p. 261.

14 Charlotte Benton and Tim Benton, 'The Style and the Age', in *Art Deco*, ed. Benton et al., p. 13.

15 Both reviews are collected in François Lesure, *Igor Stravinsky, 'Le Sacre du printemps': Dossier de presse* (Geneva, 1980), trans. and quoted in Stuart Campbell, 'Stravinsky and the Critics', in *The Cambridge Companion to Stravinsky*, ed. Jonathan Cross (Cambridge, 2003), pp. 239, 237.

16 Olin Downes, quoted in Mark N. Grant, *Maestros of the Pen: A History of Classical Music Criticism in America* (Boston, MA, 1998), p. 269.

17 See Richard Davenport-Hines, *A Night at the Majestic: Proust and the Great Modernist Dinner Party of 1922* (London, 2006), especially chapter Seven.

18 Ibid., p. 6.

19 Boris Asaf'yev, *A Book about Stravinsky*, trans. Richard F. French (Ann Arbor, MI, 1982), p. 6.

20 Milan Kundera, 'Improvisation in Homage to Stravinsky', in *Testaments Betrayed*, trans. Linda Asher (London, 1995), pp. 96–8.

21 Quoted in Scott Messing, *Neoclassicism in Music: From the Genesis of the Concept through the Schoenberg/Stravinsky Polemic* (Rochester, NY, 1988), p. 130.
22 Davis, 'Chanel, Stravinsky, and Musical Chic', p. 452.

6 To the Glory of God

1 Boris Asaf'yev, *A Book about Stravinsky*, trans. Richard F. French (Ann Arbor, MI, 1982), p. 264.
2 Stephen Walsh, *The Music of Stravinsky* (Oxford, 1988), p. 148.
3 See Graham Griffiths, *Stravinsky's Piano: Genesis of a Musical Language* (Cambridge, 2013).
4 Tamara Levitz, *Modernist Mysteries: 'Perséphone'* (New York, 2012), p. 331.
5 See ibid., p. 157.
6 Richard Taruskin, *Stravinsky and the Russian Traditions: A Biography of the Works through 'Mavra'* (Oxford, 1996), p. 1618.

7 An Extraordinary Creative Partnership: Stravinsky and Balanchine

1 Some of these details are recounted in Charles M. Joseph, *Stravinsky and Balanchine: A Journey of Invention* (New Haven, CT, 2002), pp. 45–6, transcribed from out-takes from Tony Palmer's film.
2 See, for example, Stephanie Jordan, *Stravinsky's Dances: Re-visions Across a Century* (Alton, Hampshire, 2007), especially chapter Three.
3 George Balanchine, 'The Dance Element in Stravinsky's Music', in *Stravinsky in the Theatre*, ed. Minna Lederman (New York, 1949), p. 78.
4 Igor Stravinsky and Robert Craft, *Memories and Commentaries* (London, 1960, reprinted 1981), p. 37.
5 Léon Bakst, 'The Paths of Classicism in Art', trans. and introd. by Robert Johnson, *Dance Chronicle*, XIII/2 (1990), pp. 170–92.
6 See Sjeng Scheijen, *Diaghilev: A Life*, trans. Jane Hedley-Prôle and S. J. Leinbach (London, 2009), p. 173.

7 Balanchine, 'The Dance Element in Stravinsky's Music', p. 81.

8 Paul Griffiths, *Stravinsky* (New York, 1993), p. 98.

9 Igor Stravinsky, *Poetics of Music in the Form of Six Lessons*, trans. Arthur Knodel and Ingolf Dahl (Cambridge, MA, 1947, first published in French as *Poétique musicale*, 1942), pp. 80–81.

10 George Steiner, quoted by Edward Said, 'Reflections on Exile', in *Altogether Elsewhere: Writers on Exile*, ed. Marc Robinson (San Diego, CA, 1994), p. 137.

11 Said, 'Reflections on Exile', p. 143.

8 Another War, Another Country

1 Stephen Walsh, *The Music of Stravinsky* (Oxford, 1988), p. 176.

9 An Opera About Opera

1 *Houston Post* (26 January 1949), quoted in Robert Craft, '"Dear Bob[sky]" (Stravinsky's Letters to Robert Craft, 1944–1949)', *Musical Quarterly*, LXV/3 (1979), p. 424.

2 David Bindman, *Hogarth* (London, 1981), p. 55.

3 Robert Craft, *Stravinsky: Chronicle of a Friendship* (revd and expanded edn, Nashville, TN, 1994), p. 22.

4 Aldous Huxley, *The Doors of Perception* (London, 1954, reprinted 1977), p. 19.

5 John Fuller, *W. H. Auden: A Commentary* (London, 1998), p. 437.

6 Igor Stravinsky and Robert Craft, *Memories and Commentaries* (London, 1960, reprinted 1981), p. 157.

7 Johan Huizinga, *Homo Ludens: A Study of the Play Element in Culture* (Boston, MA, 1955; first published in Dutch in 1938), p. 211.

8 W. H. Auden, *'The Dyer's Hand' and Other Essays* (London, 1963), p. 473.

9 Svetlana Boym, *The Future of Nostalgia* (New York, 2001), p. 8.

10 A Crisis and a Way Forward

1 Richard Taruskin, 'Stravinsky and the Subhuman', in *Defining Russia Musically* (Princeton, NJ, 1997), pp. 454–60.

11 A Citizen of the Modern World

1 After an account of the 'Master Mechanic' (no author credited), *Time*, LII/4 (26 July 1948), pp. 26–9.
2 Jean Cocteau, 'Stravinsky Stop-Press', 1924 appendix to 'Cock and Harlequin', in Cocteau, *A Call to Order*, trans. Rollo H. Myers (New York, 1974), pp. 61–2.
3 Robert Craft, *Stravinsky: Chronicle of a Friendship* (revd and expanded edn, Nashville, TN, 1994), p. 9.
4 See Valérie Dufour, *Stravinski et ses exégètes (1910–1940)* (Brussels, 2006).
5 See Stephen Walsh on Craft, in *Stravinsky: Second Exile. France and America, 1934–1971* (London, 2006), pp. 419–26.
6 For a sophisticated discussion of this event in context, see Mark Carroll, *Music and Ideology in Cold War Europe* (Cambridge, 2003).
7 Craft, *Stravinsky: Chronicle of a Friendship*, p. 329.
8 André Boucourechliev, *Stravinsky*, trans. Martin Cooper (London, 1987), p. 304.
9 Louis Andriessen and Elmer Schönberger, *The Apollonian Clockwork: On Stravinsky*, trans. Jeff Hamburg (Oxford, 1989, first published in Dutch in 1983), p. 265; republished by Amsterdam University Press (2006).

Postlude: Stravinsky Remains

1 'Une lettre de Tamara Nijinski', *Le Monde* (27 May 2013); a translation can be read at www.danceeurope.net (accessed 23 July 2014).
2 Pierre Boulez, 'Stravinsky Remains', in *Stocktakings from an Apprenticeship*, trans. Stephen Walsh (Oxford, 1991), pp. 55–110. The essay was first published in French in 1951.

3 Louis Andriessen and Elmer Schönberger, *The Apollonian Clockwork: On Stravinsky*, trans. Jeff Hamburg (Oxford, 1989, first published in Dutch in 1983), p. 101; republished by Amsterdam University Press (2006).

4 Ibid., p. 100.

Select Bibliography

Andriessen, Louis, and Elmer Schönberger, *The Apollonian Clockwork: On Stravinsky*, trans. Jeff Hamburg (Oxford, 1989). Republished by Amsterdam University Press (2006). First published in Dutch in 1983

Asaf'yev, Boris, *A Book about Stravinsky*, trans. Richard F. French (Ann Arbor, MI, 1982). First published in Leningrad in 1929 as *Kniga o Stravinskom* under Asaf'yev's nom de plume, Igor Glebov

Benton, Charlotte, Tim Benton and Ghislaine Wood, eds, *Art Deco, 1910–1939* (London, 2003)

Boucourechliev, André, *Stravinsky*, trans. Martin Cooper (London, 1987)

Carr, Maureen, *Stravinsky's 'Pulcinella': A Facsimile Edition of the Musical Sketches* (Middleton, WI, 2010)

—, *After the Rite: Stravinsky's Path to Neoclassicism (1914–25)* (New York, 2014)

Casella, Alfredo, *Strawinsky* (Brescia, 1947)

Cocteau, Jean, *A Call to Order*, trans. Rollo H. Myers (New York, 1974)

Corle, Edwin, ed., *Igor Stravinsky* (New York, 1949)

Craft, Robert, *Stravinsky: Chronicle of a Friendship* (Nashville, TN, revd and expanded edn 1994). First published in 1973

—, *Igor and Vera Stravinsky: A Photograph Album, 1921–1971* (London, 1982)

—, *Stravinsky: Selected Correspondence*, 3 vols (New York, 1982–5)

—, *A Stravinsky Scrapbook, 1940–1971* (London, 1983)

—, *Stravinsky: Glimpses of a Life* (New York, 1992)

—, *Down a Path of Wonder: Memoirs of Stravinsky, Schoenberg and other Cultural Figures* (n.p., 2006)

—, *Stravinsky: Discoveries and Memories* (n.p., 2013)

Cross, Jonathan, *The Stravinsky Legacy* (Cambridge, 1998)

—, ed., *The Cambridge Companion to Stravinsky* (Cambridge, 2003)

Danuser, Hermann, and Heidy Zimmermann, eds, *Avatar of Modernity: 'The Rite of Spring' Reconsidered* (London, 2013)

Davenport-Hines, Richard, *A Night at the Majestic: Proust and the Great Modernist Dinner Party of 1922* (London, 2006)

Davis, Mary E., *Classic Chic: Music, Fashion and Modernism* (Berkeley, CA, 2006)

Druskin, Mikhail, *Igor Stravinsky: His Life, Works and Views*, trans. Martin Cooper (Cambridge, 1983). First published in Russian in Leningrad in 1974

Dufour, Valérie, *Stravinski et ses exégètes (1910–1940)* (Brussels, 2006)

Figes, Orlando, *Natasha's Dance: A Cultural History of Russia* (London, 2002)

Garafola, Lynn, *Diaghilev's Ballets Russes* (New York, 1989)

Greenhalgh, Chris, *Coco and Igor* (London, 2002)

Griffiths, Graham, *Stravinsky's Piano: Genesis of a Musical Language* (Cambridge, 2013)

Griffiths, Paul, *Igor Stravinsky: 'The Rake's Progress'* (Cambridge, 1982)

—, *Stravinsky* (New York, 1993)

Grigoriev, S. L. [Sergey Leonidovich], *The Diaghilev Ballet, 1909–1929*, trans. and ed. Vera Bowen (London, 1953)

Hill, Peter, *Stravinsky: 'The Rite of Spring'* (Cambridge, 2000)

Jordan, Stephanie, *Stravinsky's Dances: Re-visions Across a Century* (Alton, Hampshire, 2007)

Joseph, Charles M., *Stravinsky Inside Out* (New Haven, CT, 2002)

—, *Stravinsky and Balanchine: A Journey of Invention* (New Haven, CT, 2002)

—, *Stravinsky's Ballets* (New Haven, CT, 2011)

Lederman, Minna, ed., *Stravinsky in the Theatre* (New York, 1949)

Levitz, Tamara, *Modernist Mysteries: 'Perséphone'* (New York, 2012)

—, ed., *Stravinsky and His World* (Princeton, NJ, 2013)

Libman, Lillian, *And Music at the Close: Stravinsky's Last Years, a Personal Memoir* (New York, 1972)

Messing, Scott, *Neoclassicism in Music: From the Genesis of the Concept through the Schoenberg/Stravinsky Polemic* (Rochester, NY, 1988)

Nabokov, Nicolas, *Igor Strawinsky* (Berlin, 1964)

Oliver, Michael, *Igor Stravinsky* (London, 1995)

Schaeffner, André, *Strawinsky* (Paris, 1931)

Scheijen, Sjeng, *Diaghilev: A Life*, trans. Jane Hedley-Prôle and S. J. Leinbach (London, 2009)

Schloezer, Boris de, *Igor Stravinsky* (Paris, 1929)

Straus, Joseph N., *Stravinsky's Late Music* (Cambridge, 2001)

Stravinsky, Igor, *An Autobiography (1903–1934)* (London, 1990). English translation first published 1936 (no translator given). Originally published in French as *Chroniques de ma vie* (Paris, 1935)

—, *Poetics of Music in the Form of Six Lessons*, trans. Arthur Knodel and Ingolf Dahl (Cambridge, MA, 1947). Originally published in French as *Poétique musicale* (Cambridge, MA, 1942)

Stravinsky, Igor, and Robert Craft, *Conversations with Igor Stravinsky* (London, 1959)

—, *Memories and Commentaries* (London, 1960, reprinted 1981)

—, *Expositions and Developments* (London, 1962, reprinted 1981)

—, *Dialogues and a Diary* (Garden City, NY, 1963)

—, *The Rite of Spring Sketches, 1911–1913* (London, 1969)

—, *Themes and Conclusions* (London, 1972)

Stravinsky, Vera, and Robert Craft, *Stravinsky in Pictures and Documents* (London, 1979)

Strawinsky, Théodore and Denise, *Au coeur du foyer: Catherine et Igor Strawinsky, 1906–1940* (Bourg-la-Reine, 1998), trans. by Stephen Walsh as *Stravinsky: A Family Chronicle* (London, 2004)

Taruskin, Richard, *Stravinsky and the Russian Traditions: A Biography of the Works through 'Mavra'* (Oxford, 1996)

—, *Defining Russia Musically* (Princeton, NJ, 1997)

Vlad, Roman, *Stravinsky*, trans. Frederick and Ann Fuller (London, 3rd paperback edn, 1985). First published in Rome in Italian in 1958

Walsh, Stephen, *The Music of Stravinsky* (Oxford, 1988)

—, *Stravinsky: 'Oedipus Rex'* (Cambridge, 1993)

—, *Igor Stravinsky: A Creative Spring. Russia and France, 1882–1934* (London, 2000)

—, *Stravinsky: Second Exile. France and America, 1934–1971* (London, 2006)

Watkins, Glenn, *Pyramids at the Louvre: Music, Culture, and Collage from Stravinsky to the Postmodernists* (Cambridge, MA, 1994)

White, Eric Walter, *Stravinsky: The Composer and His Works* (London, 2nd edn, 1979)

Select Discography and Videography

The recorded legacy of Stravinsky's music is vast, beginning with his own 'recordings' in the early 1920s of original works and arrangements for piano roll, and his first recordings as conductor of his Russian ballet scores in the late 1920s. He went on to record key works many times across his working life. The most comprehensive edition of recordings made by the composer and Robert Craft of works from the early Symphony in E-flat to the late *The Owl and the Pussy-cat* is the 22-CD set *Works of Igor Stravinsky* (Sony 88697103112, 2007). This is a reissue of *Stravinsky: The Recorded Legacy*, a 31-LP set released in 1982 for the centenary of the composer's birth.

The CD and DVD recordings listed below (in chronological order of date of release) are just a small handful of notable interpretations of Stravinsky's music.

Movements for Piano and Orchestra: Moscow Conservatoire Orchestra, Sviatoslav Richter, Yuri Nikolaevsky (Russian Revelation 10093, 1998)

Sonata for Two Pianos; Concerto for Two Pianos; *The Rite of Spring* (four-hand version): Benjamin Frith, Peter Hill (Naxos 8553386, 2000)

Oedipus Rex: Jessye Norman, Philip Langridge, Bryn Terfel, Saito Kinen Orchestra, Seiji Ozawa (Philips DVD Video 0743077, 2005)

'Stravinsky Plays Stravinsky: Masters of the Piano Roll', including Piano Sonata: (Dal Segno DSPRCD007, 2005)

'Stravinsky 125th Anniversary Album': Violin Concerto; *Zvezdolikiy*; *Symphonies of Wind Instruments*; *The Rite of Spring*: Jennifer Frautschi, Orchestra of St Luke's, Philharmonia Orchestra, Robert Craft (Naxos 8557508, 2007)

Symphony in C; *Symphony of Psalms*; Symphony in Three Movements: Rundfunkchor Berlin, Berliner Philharmoniker, Sir Simon Rattle (EMI 2076300, 2008)

'Stravinsky in Moscow 1962', including *Fireworks; Petrushka* suite; *Ode*; *Orpheus*: Moscow State Philharmonic Orchestra, USSR State Symphony Orchestra, Igor Stravinsky (Melodiya MELCD1001604, 2009)

'Boulez Conducts Stravinsky': 6-CD set (DG 4778730, 2010)

'Music Dances: Balanchine Choreographs Stravinsky', including danced excerpts from *Apollo*, *Agon*, etc. (George Balanchine Foundation DVD Video, 2010)

The Rake's Progress (David Hockney designer, John Cox director): Miah Persson, Topi Lehtipuu, Matthew Rose, Glyndebourne Chorus, London Philharmonic Orchestra, Vladimir Jurowski (Opus Arte DVD Video OA1062D, 2011)

'Stravinsky–Ansermet: The First Decca Recordings', including *Firebird* suite, 1949, and *The Rite of Spring*, 1950 (Australian Eloquence ELQ4803775, 2012)

Firebird suite, *The Rite of Spring*: historic first recordings conducted by Stravinsky in the late 1920s (Pristine Audio Pasc387, 2013)

Les Noces, and other choral works: New London Chamber Choir, New London Chamber Ensemble, The Voronezh Chamber Choir, James Wood (Helios CDH55467, 2014)

Le Sacre du printemps, *Petrushka*: Les Siècles, François-Xavier Roth (Actes Sud ASM15, 2014)

Acknowledgements

I owe a huge debt of gratitude to Martha Jay at Reaktion Books for first suggesting I write this Critical Life, and for her undying patience in waiting for it. My thanks also go to Susannah Jayes and Aimee Selby at Reaktion for their kind support.

My wish for *Igor Stravinsky*, in the spirit of the series in which it sits, is that it offer a new critical take on the extraordinary life, times and music of its subject. Nonetheless, it rides in the wake of the substantial number of biographies that have gone before it. Two recent studies in particular have reshaped for the twenty-first century the understanding of this celebrated composer of the twentieth century: the landscape-changing *Stravinsky and the Russian Traditions* by Richard Taruskin (1996) and the comprehensive two volumes of the biography by Stephen Walsh (1999 and 2006). Without their painstaking scholarship my own work would simply not have been possible.

The kindness and generosity of so many friends and colleagues, in so many different ways, have helped make the book so much better than it would otherwise have been: David Allenby at Boosey & Hawkes, Rosamund Bartlett, Joanna Bullivant, Olga Carbin for supervising my slow progress with the Russian language, Maureen Carr, Eric Clarke, Alice Cross, Emma Cross, John and Margaret Cross, Rebecca Cross, Laurence Dreyfus, David Gallagher, Graham Griffiths, Paul Griffiths for his support and encouragement as well as for saving me from the public embarrassment of far too many shameful gaffes, Julian Johnson, Tamara Levitz, Ann McKay, Peter McMullin, Gillian Moore, Ulrich Mosch, Caroline Palmer at the Ashmolean Museum, and Jim Samson, plus the patient help of the staff of the Paul Sacher Stiftung, Basel, and of the Bodleian, Christ Church and Music Faculty libraries at the University of Oxford.

I am very grateful for a grant from the OUP/John Fell Fund of the University of Oxford, which bought me valuable writing time when I most needed it.

Photo Acknowledgements

The author and the publishers wish to express their thanks to the below sources of illustrative material and/or permission to reproduce it:

Alamy: pp. 30 (The Art Archive), 86, 95 (RIA Novosti), 108 (Photos 12); Arnold Newman: p. 140; Bridgeman Images: p. 22 (Ashmolean Museum, University of Oxford); Corbis: pp. 17 (Bettmann), 77 (Leemage), 81 (Hulton-Deutsch Collection), 149 (Jerry Cooke), 172 (Marvin Koner); Jean-Pierre Dalbéra: p. 90; Dutch National Archives, The Hague: p. 186; Getty Images: p. 127 (Sasha); © David Hockney/photo credit: Richard Schmidt/Collection The David Hockney Foundation: p. 156; Library of Congress, Washington, DC: pp. 6, 9; Nicholas Roerich Museum: p. 57; Pline: p. 89; Rex Shutterstock: p. 58 (Alastair Muir); Shutterstock: p. 25 (irisphoto1).